Unleash
your
creativity

Unleash your creativity

52 brilliant ideas for creative genius

Rob Bevan and Tim Wright

brilliantideas

First published in 2005 by
The Infinite Ideas Company Limited
36 St Giles
Oxford
OX1 3LD
United Kingdom
www.infideas.com

Reprinted 2007

A CIP catalogue record for this book is available from the British Library.

ISBN 978-1-904902-17-1

Designed and typeset by Baseline Arts Ltd, Oxford
Printed and bound by TJ International, Cornwall

Brilliant ideas

Brilliant features

Each chapter of this book is designed to provide you with an inspirational idea that you can read quickly and put into practice straight away.

Throughout you'll find four features that will help you to get right to the heart of the idea:

- *Try another idea* If this idea looks like a life-changer then there's no time to lose. *Try another idea* will point you straight to a related tip to expand and enhance the first.

- *Here's an idea for you* Give it a go – right here, right now – and get an idea of how well you're doing so far.

- *Defining ideas* Words of wisdom from masters and mistresses of the art, plus some interesting hangers-on.

- *How did it go?* If at first you do succeed try to hide your amazement. If, on the other hand, you don't this is where you'll find a Q and A that highlights common problems and how to get over them.

Introduction

If you've just picked up this book, chances are the first thing you want to hear is that anyone can be creative. Well, you're right.

We don't believe creativity is something you're born with, like brown eyes or blond hair – it's something we're *all* born with. We all began life with the ability to play, to experiment, to examine things until they break and then to throw tantrums when we weren't able to change the world around us. Trouble is, many of us forget that creativity has its roots in these childhood abilities and that growing out of them doesn't just stifle our inner child, it stifles our creativity.

The second thing you'd probably like us to say is that being creative is easy. It isn't. Creativity is hard work, or at least something you need to work hard at. Recognising that you need to apply the same discipline to your creative life as you do to what you normally think of as work is a big step to becoming more creative. Knowing what you want to do and then what you have to do to make it happen is one big difference between adult creativity and child's play. This realisation means that next time you get the urge to change the world around you, instead of just throwing a tantrum like a child, you'll have the means to do so.

But if this is all beginning to sound like too much hard work, we've also got some great suggestions about how to make work seem more like play. If there's one thing this book sets out to convince you of, it's this: you need to take your playtime more seriously *and* have more fun at work.

We've got some basic strategies for 'thinking creatively', the sort of things you'd expect in a book like this, coupled with some new ways of looking at everyday tasks that most people don't think of as being creative at all, like research. Most of these are techniques we employ every day, so we know they work. And we've got plenty of examples of how they've worked for other people too.

In a field where usually 'anything goes', many of these involve placing restrictions and imposing arbitrary rules on your activities, often for no good reason. Sometimes being creative means being deliberately obtuse, doing the unexpected, surprising others and yourself, by seeking out the unfashionable and turning your back on your own successes.

Sometimes creativity really is a force you can 'unleash'. Understanding the value of being systematically destructive as well as inventive, finding equivalents for physical acts of creative abandon in our increasingly virtual world and learning to love the resulting screw-ups are all part of the process.

At other times the process needs to be more deliberate, more controlled, like the precise application of the right tool at the right time. Organising your creative toolbox is essential, even if the best results sometimes come from picking the wrong tool for the job or swapping tools with somebody else. In our minds, toolbox is synonymous with toybox, so along the way we hope you'll also treat yourself to some new toys as well.

And while you're at it, treat yourself to some new friends too. Traditionally, creativity has been seen as a solitary activity, best characterised by the artistic loner working for years in isolation and poverty. Nowadays, we work in creative 'industries', and collaboration is not only essential – it's the best way to succeed. It's not just the business community that needs to spend time networking.

You'll find many references in this book to that other network, the internet, and to technology in general. This is partly because this is the medium in which we work, but also because we think this is where some of the most interesting creative work is happening. Don't be afraid to be a geek: like it or not, technology is ubiquitous and here to stay, and we think creative people should be the first to embrace technology, not the last, albeit with a healthy dose of irony and scepticism.

But don't spend too much time working on your 'monitor tan'; we all need get away from our screens and get out more. We'll give you some ideas about how to maximise the creative opportunities of travel, whether you're looping aimlessly around your neighbourhood, delivering off-the-cuff waffle on the international conference circuit or holidaying with your family.

Finally, just as we needed to stop writing this book so that we could get it in your hands, it's important to know when to stop, to come back in the morning with fresh ideas, or just to spend time doing absolutely nothing. But not right now. This is the beginning of the book, not the end. Don't even think about stopping here. Go on – start anywhere, start now!

1

Start anywhere, start now

How to start being creative with the things around you, right here, right now, no excuses, no prevarication.

Not knowing when or how to begin is a problem we're all quite familiar with. It may well be the reason why you're reading this.

For many people, taking that first step is the most difficult aspect of any creative task. It's a declaration of intent and also an act of faith, since all too often we start a project without really knowing where to start or – worryingly – where, how or when it will end.

Sometimes, too, getting started can feel like the end of a lovely period of free and endless thinking. Giving shape and form to your ideas can feel like you're killing them a little, selling them short – or limiting them in some way that feels uncomfortable.

Certainly when we sat down to write this book knowing where to start was a bit of a problem. And we had even greater problems building up the head of steam that would actually get us going.

It's amazing, in fact, how creative one can be when it comes to finding ways of *not* starting. Rob, for example, often feels the need to clear his desk of all distractions,

Here's an idea for you...

If you need proof of how pregnant with creative possibility 'found' objects can be, take a look at www.foundmagazine.com. You're almost bound to find something there that can become your jumping off point for a new idea.

to have gathered together all possible source materials close to hand, and possibly even to have installed all the latest software upgrades before he can do anything. Tim will usually engross himself in a series of seemingly urgent household chores, including laundry, washing up, gardening and supermarket shopping.

These may look like avoidance techniques, but your supposed creativity experts (that's us, by the way) are here to tell you that a fair deal of vital mental and emotional preparation goes on during this time. Tim's wife refers to this process (somewhat sardonically, it has to be admitted) as 'sharpening pencils'.

To some extent, how you delay and prepare yourself for the task ahead may well help reveal the best way in to your work. Sometimes you really do have to sneak up on your ideas and view them from several angles before deciding on your point of attack.

It is not always the best approach to start at the beginning. This idea, for example, was written more than halfway through the project. Quite often, you need to get to the point where you can see the whole of the project and understand the style of the piece before you can deliver an opening that really sets it all off.

Sometimes you tackle the most difficult and challenging problem first. Usually this is because you've already sussed out how to solve it, or you're so bursting with energy and excitement that you need something major to attack.

On the other hand, peripheral matters can often be good starting points, because they can be done easily and quickly. There's a lot to be said for getting something done, even if it's small.

Quite *when* you start is a different matter – and usually depends on what your brief is. Much of the time, your creative work will be about addressing a specific problem within a specific time frame. That makes it easier to give yourself some deadlines to work to and a plan of action. But starting with a completely blank canvas and no particular brief changes the rules (a bit), and much depends on the resources you have to hand.

So pause from reading for a moment and take stock of all the things that are lying around you right now. If you're an organised person, you may well have a whole heap of really useful research material and tools ready and waiting. If you're not organised, you probably still have a whole heap of really useful research material and tools ready and waiting, but you just don't know it yet.

This book is very much about looking at everyday things in a different light and putting them to use in unusual ways. So don't ever think that you have nothing to get started with. Just use what you can find.

It's easy to get started if you have a whole load of materials to turn to. Collecting stuff, making notes and taking photos can provide you with plenty of creative stimulation. Look at IDEA 2, *Do your research.*

Try another idea...

'The brain is a wonderful organ; it starts the moment you get up in the morning and does not stop until you get to the office.'
ROBERT FROST

Defining idea...

How did
it go?

Q **My problem is not the starting, but knowing where to finish and how to give my creative ramblings some structure and shape. What would you suggest?**

A *Well, I suppose as well as 'begin anywhere', we could tell you to 'finish nowhere'. And there is a school of thought that suggests that no work of art is really finished, but has simply been interrupted at some point in its making. Then there's the rather 'Zen' approach to finishing described by T.S. Eliot: 'We shall not cease from exploration/ And the end of all our exploring/ Will be to arrive where we started/ And know the place for the first time.' The truth is, you can finish anywhere. The work stops when you decide to stop it. Remember too you could always hand your work over to someone else to finish – their distance from the work could give them a clearer view of what works and what doesn't.*

Q **I spent the whole day sharpening pencils and tidying my desktop and made no progress on my project. What should I do tomorrow?**

A *Sometimes these kinds of activities help clear your mind of other distractions, allowing you to focus on the problem at hand, but in your case it sounds like they ARE just avoidance techniques. If you haven't actually spent any time thinking about your project, the chances are you'll just have another bad day. Try and think of one single thing, anything, you can do to progress your project. If that doesn't help break the deadlock, maybe it's time to work on something else.*

2

Do your research

When studying any new subject it's important to learn when to skim and when to take the plunge and dive in deep.

Over time you can develop the kind of instinct that will help you effectively sift and sort everything that comes your way.

When we talk about research here, we don't just mean long hours in the library or on the internet, boning up on a specialist subject like the history of liquorice or advanced bauxite mining techniques. That's the kind of research that happens when you already know what you're doing creatively, and you're attacking your interest in an organised, methodical way. If you're genuinely interested in a single subject area, the best thing to do – even in these days of the Web and multiple information sources – is get hold of a couple of authoritative books.

But what research should you be doing when you don't know what you're looking for? The fact is that creative people are always curious, always on the lookout for new stimuli and therefore always researching in one way or another. It's therefore important to develop a sense of curiosity about everything that confronts you. Be vigilant. Ask 'why' a lot. Don't accept anything at face value.

Cross-referencing and linking your research – either deliberately or at random – is a fantastic way to get started with new ideas. Ask yourself: 'What links the last three books I've read?' Or pick three areas you've looked at quite separately – say, cooking, code and collage – jam them together and see what kind of relationship your imagination can forge between them.

One easy way to engage in this process of constant research is to keep a camera handy (preferably digital) and take photos of everything and anything that catches your eye. Another is to squirrel away little bits of information (and intriguing bits of rubbish!) as you find them, building up a personal collection of seemingly useless and unrelated factoids, newspaper cuttings, URL bookmarks, postcards, brochures, food packaging... anything that catches your eye. This process is sometimes referred to as 'jackdawing'.

Be careful, though: unless you are wise to the next great trick of good creative research – knowing when to ignore something you come across – you'll end up with a house (or tree, for the serious squirrels among you) full of rubbish or more photos than you could fit on Mount Fuji.

'I find that a great part of the information I have was acquired by looking up something and finding something else on the way.'
FRANKLIN ADAMS, writer

So how do you know when something you've stumbled across is worth keeping, exploring or even incorporating into your creative output? And how can you tell when the rubbish you're rifling through is just that – rubbish? Frankly, you probably don't, not right away. You simply have to develop your own instinct and work on hunches.

If that sounds like a cop-out on our part, always ask yourself whenever you're picking up on something for this first time: how confident am I that the effort I'm investing in this X is going to be rewarded with some kind of creative output? In short, how excited and stimulated do you feel about the creative possibilities of X?

The Web is great for detailed delving into a specialist subject or for random searching for strange new creative stimuli. Learn how to 'googlewhack' in IDEA 47, *Get Googling*.

Try another idea...

Some intriguing items only need to be looked at once to be logged. You don't need to take things any further. You've simply picked out a nugget from the dross. But other sources of inspiration may require further inspection. You've simply uncovered the first signs of a rich seam that you now need to explore more thoroughly.

At this point you may need to consider your prospecting/mining techniques. Do you sift through things in fine detail or blast away at big chunks of the research landscape with a stick of dynamite? Both approaches are valid. Sifting gives you a good chance of picking up even more nuggets that you weren't expecting to find (and which may take you off on a tangent into a completely different area of research). Blasting may expose not just one seam, but many, thus encouraging you to keep digging and not curtail your research at the first sign of success.

'For some reason I'm interested in liquorice at the moment but no other root based herb or confectionary.'
ROB

Defining idea...

7

What's important here is that your collection can become an inventory of the things that interest you; and consequently you are defining to some extent the scope and range of your work. Don't feel hemmed in by this. You'll still be able to synthesise your research materials in any number of ways, with magical results.

How did it go?

Q   I'm doing the research, but it's not inspiring me. Where can I find that spark?

A   *Remember not to always mine in the same place each time. Don't rely on the same sources for all your research materials: go to a different library, surf a different area of the Web; hang out with a different set of experts. To close off the mining metaphor (finally), if you keep digging in the same place either your seam is going to run dry or you'll end up making the same discoveries over and over again.*

Q   There still seems to be so much to master about my chosen research area. Where and when will it end?

A   *It will end whenever and wherever you want it to. Sure, it's great to build up your expertise. But being creative isn't always about being an expert or a completist. No one's ever going to give you a formal test about what you do or don't know (are they?). Everything you're learning is for your benefit only – and that's what makes this kind of research really liberating.*

3

Know your own history

If you can learn how to repeat good tricks and be aware of traditions in creativity, you'll end up working faster *and* smarter.

To a large extent everything you ever do in your creative life can be seen as a reaction to the things you've done before.

Sometimes it's a gentle refinement of previous ideas or working practices, sometimes it's a full-scale revolt against all that has gone before. Either way, if you're not aware of your past and the cultural heritage from which you are drawing, you'll be in severe danger of repeating mistakes endlessly, and never really developing your creative skills.

Every time you start a new project, try looking back over past work and picking key elements that reveal themselves as your standard working devices. Pick up, too, on key themes that keep coming back to haunt you. Ask yourself: 'What works for me about that? Why am I so interested in that kind of thing, those characters, objects, colours…?' If you inspect your past work like this regularly, you'll always be starting a new piece of work from a position of self-knowledge. And decisions about what to accept or reject from your creative past will be that much more solid.

Here's an idea for you... **Replay the same scenes with different consequences. Shakespeare did this with similar characters in different plays (ambitious usurpers, jealous lovers, foolish kings, parted lovers), and the different consequences led to very different drama. Could you take four or five generic elements of your creative work and keep replaying them in different configurations like this?**

One benefit of cataloguing and coming to terms with your own strengths and weaknesses is that you'll learn to achieve simple effects much more quickly. And if some of the standard elements of what you're doing are easily repeatable, you'll have more time to concentrate on the new. In this way, ideas can be like software libraries.

Stand-up comedians do the same thing in building up libraries of jokes and stories. It's not that they're planning to do the same schtick every night (although some of them do). Rather, they want to have a broad range of material to draw upon when reacting to a specific situation, audience or heckler – and want to know than the material has been road-tested and works. Comedians also often have signature routines or catchphrases that their audience come to expect – or even demand – them to perform. For the successful stand-up the battle is to play with this familiarity, dropping in the catchphrase or joke at different points in the show, with a twist or in a slightly different context.

Some comedians are very good at understanding the deeper traditions of their craft and bone up on successful performers from previous generations. For example, Lee Evans in the 1990s owed a great debt to Norman Wisdom's routines from the 1950s – but was no less funny or contemporary because of that. Old wine in new bottles can still taste good.

Defining idea... **'Style is self-plagiarism.'**
ALFRED HITCHCOCK

People like Evans have broadened this lesson about knowing your own history and have benefited from knowing other people's. The key is to be comfortable with the idea of history repeating itself, but to remain critical about its value. Indeed, there can be something almost scientific about setting up the same parameters in a series of experiments and observing if the same outcomes occur. Very often they don't – or at least there are some fascinating variations and nuances. No two plants will grow exactly the same in the same soil. Think of Cézanne painting fruit or Rembrandt painting himself over and over again, each time revealing something different about the object they paint, as well as about themselves and their painting technique.

You could try doing this in your own life. Tomorrow, try and do exactly the same things as you did today at exactly the same time of day and for the same period of time. Note the similarities and differences in terms of how the day actually unfolds and the different feelings each day elicits. If you can get away with it, try repeating this for a whole week. By day seven, how do you think you'll feel? Terminally bored or creatively inspired? Probably a little bit of both, no?

Quite often it is tempting *not* to repeat good tricks because you want to try something new or unknown. It may work – but it may fall flat. Try IDEA 9, *Make more mistakes faster*.

Try another idea...

'Always dream and shoot higher than you know how to. Don't bother just to be better than your contemporaries or predecessors. Try to be better than yourself.'
WILLIAM FAULKNER

Defining idea...

How did it go?

Q   I'm not sure I've been working long enough to have my own particular style. How can I improve?

A   *Perhaps you're thinking too narrowly about your creative output. Think about your creative style in terms of your relations with others, the banter, the jokes, and think about what you do that goes down best and with whom.*

Q   I know my own history all too well, but that doesn't mean I can break free of it creatively. What should I try?

A   *Sometimes the problem lies in the way your history revolves around other people, who themselves are trapped in a cycle of endlessly repeating themselves without knowing it. For example, an aspect of the comic tradition is the number of highly successful double acts there have been (not true in, say, literature or fine art). A lot of what an audience enjoys about the great double acts – Laurel & Hardy, Abbot & Costello, Morecombe & Wise – is the repetition, the stereotypical behaviour of the straight man and his clownish partner, the same dynamic between the two being explored over and over again, quite often using the same language and with same outcome: the pratfall, the public humiliation, the custard pie. In this scenario, the creative value – the comedy – is entirely wrapped up in everyone knowing implicitly the 'history' between the two people. This may be something to consider in your own creative collaborations. Are you aware of the patterns of behaviour and mental routines you fall into when working with particular people? When you have creative meetings, are the outcomes predictable? Are they comfortable? Are they satisfying?*

4

Be organised

Keeping a tidy desk and writing out long, neat to-do lists are all very well. But how can you be sure that you're going to end the day having really *done* something?

A big part of being creative is not simply about being 'inspired', it's about getting things done. So join the art and graft movement.

Since we all became 'knowledge workers' of one kind or another – and increasingly time-poor as a result – time management has become a whole industry in itself. The world is infested with time-management devices, theories and techniques to make them work. But don't be fooled by this. Above all, don't panic-buy the latest newfangled kit and associated manuals that will ultimately do you no good. We're here to tell you that at the core of all of this time-management mumbo-jumbo lies just one essential device: the good old-fashioned to-do list.

Whatever you use to create your to-do list – be it a piece of scrap paper, post-it notes, a white board or a PDA – the basic principles are the same. You need to concentrate on three things.

Write a list of impossible tasks. Put it away somewhere safe and only get it out at the end of a day if you're completely overwhelmed, or you feel you haven't really achieved what you set out to do. Looking at it might help you regain a sense of perspective and become re-energised for tomorrow.

1. smart and realistic prioritisation of the tasks

2. the breaking down of big tasks into smaller, more achievable ones

3. the making of a new list for every new day

When it comes to prioritising, remember Pareto's principle, or the '80/20 rule': 80% of all results come from 20% of all efforts. This means that roughly one in five of the items on your list are truly essential and you should concentrate on completing these. Everything else may be useful, but the world won't end if they don't get done.

Don't confine yourself to simple A, B, C-style rankings of importance, however: you also need to recognise that some tasks take longer than others. For example, one 'A' category phone call might take just five minutes while an equivalent writing task could take as much as five hours.

Defining idea...

'Failing to plan is a plan to fail.'
EFFIE JONES, author

If you have one big important thing that needs to be done by the end of the day ('Send hard copy of manuscript to publisher'), be aware that a dozen smaller tasks are hidden within that one bald statement ('Check the printer works, check there is enough paper, print out the manuscript, proof-read, make revisions, print out fresh copy, bind/staple, write covering letter, buy large envelopes and stamps, check and write address, check time of the last post...and send!'). Each one of these smaller tasks needs to be itemised and allocated time. If you don't do this, how can you ever be sure that your one big to-do item of the day is really achievable?

Sometimes, your list will become just too cluttered with tasks, big and small. To combat this, make two separate lists: one of things you *absolutely* need to do today and another of things you might get round to if you have the time or inclination. Don't even think about looking at the second list until the first has been dealt with.

The end of each working day is an important time. It's then that you should compile your lists for tomorrow. Don't wait until morning and find that the first task on your new to-do list is writing a to-do list. And don't just re-edit today's list – start afresh each time.

Computers are great for reorganising lists, archiving and keeping track of the things you've done. Check out IDEA 3, *Know your own history.*

Try another idea...

Nothing beats crossing things off a paper list, or scribbling notes as you go. But hide the list – don't let it constantly remind you of the things you haven't yet done. To avoid feeling oppressed, go to IDEA 49, *Come back in the morning.*

and another...

Quite often people use up the last half hour of their working day tidying up and 'clearing the decks' for the next day. Don't. It's much better to greet the new day with a messy desk and a clear head than the other way round.

How did it go?

Q I never seem to be able to close off a task or a project. Why is there always something more to do?

A *Try every possible way of completing a task on your to-do list. When you come to each item on your list make sure you either deal with it there and then, get someone else to do it (some big corporations refer to this kind of delegation as 'push-back'), delete it altogether or, as a last resort only, put it off until later. Don't be tempted to put it off until you've tried all the other options.*

Q I'm great at making lists, but they never seem to help get things done. Why not?

A *Don't mistake list-making for doing. Too much time spent making or reviewing lists is a big time waster. Spend no more than half an hour at the end of each day planning for tomorrow.*

Q Every task I set myself always seems to take twice as long as I thought it would. Why?

A *Most things you succeed in doing will inevitably require follow-up and result in a new set of to-do tasks. When you have done something, always ask yourself: 'So what do I need to do next?' There might be things that you can safely defer until a later date, but don't let that stop you putting them on your next to-do list.*

5

Create arbitrary rules

By applying your own illogical constraints, you can quickly discover creative ways of bending the rules imposed on you by other people.

The simplest way to impose a constraint on your creativity is to give yourself a deadline.

Sure, this isn't necessarily arbitrary, since there may be good reasons for finishing a piece of work within a fixed period of time – other people may be depending on you, and it's more than likely there's money riding on the job. But even when you don't have a strict deadline, it's tempting to give yourself one anyway.

When starting with a blank sheet (literally or figuratively) give yourself just 30 minutes to work up some ideas and then force yourself to go with what you've got at that point. This is a great way of stopping yourself from over-developing or over-refining (or over-indulging) your ideas – or trying to pack too much into one activity or framework. Just because you have lots of great ideas doesn't mean you have to deal with them all at the same time. Keep some back for later.

Here's an idea for you...

Play an arbitrary game of cards. Deal each other a random number of cards and then simply make up rules on the fly about when to discard, when to pick up, when to swap cards, what constitutes a winning hand, etc. Take it in turns to add one arbitrary rule at a time and see how long you can carry on playing without the whole thing collapsing or blows being exchanged. Call each other's bluff about seemingly invalid turns and transgressions. That way you'll have to explain the game to each other and – who knows – you may actually end up inventing something you can play again as a proper game!

As well as rules for your outputs, think about silly regimes for absorbing new material. For example, Marshall McLuhan made it a rule to read only left-hand pages, but why not read only the first forty pages of any book you pick up? Or go one better and open two books at random, both at page 40, and force yourself to develop some new ideas based only on what you read on those two pages.

Rules are about patterns too. One definition of human intelligence could be our ability to detect patterns in everything we perceive. Equally, one could define human creativity as our ability to arbitrarily impose patterns on a seemingly disorderly world.

So this business of rule-making is really a very practical way of forcing yourself to think in cycles, to work with sequences, to record your own tendencies, to define behaviours and calculate probabilities – all key skills for the creative person.

It's also teaching you to be at home with the rules of randomness and gambling. The composer John Cage often used the rolling of a die to help make decisions about the composition of his music. (He also decided to become an expert in mushrooms, because 'mushroom' sat next to 'music' in the dictionary.)

As well as restricting your development methods and sources of inspiration, try restricting yourself in terms of what you actually create. See IDEA 7, *Restrict your choices to broaden your possibilities.*

Try another idea...

Being arbitrary is a great way to kick-start processes generally. Quite often designers will choose the font for a new company's logo simply by taking the first letter of the company's name and then finding a font with a name that also starts with the same letter (though not many Z-companies use ZapfDingbats, oddly enough).

It can also be helpful to give yourself some kind of regular quirk or idiosyncratic rule that becomes your own trademark. For example, Alfred Hitchcock often made a cameo appearance in his films. The film editor Walter Murch does his editing standing up (and his thinking lying down). For our part, Rob always places an aubergine somewhere in his interactive work. And Tim always wears a fez when he writes. For no good reason at all.

'Read only Left-Hand Pages: Marshall McLuhan did this. By decreasing the amount of information, we leave room for what he called our "noodle".'
BRUCE MAU, designer

Defining idea...

How did it go?

Q **Imposing meaningless rules seems to turn everything I do into a silly game. Is that normal?**

A *Yes, this can happen. But silly games can teach us a lot about serious creative business. Perhaps even more importantly, you might want to think about why you're afraid to turn your work into a silly game – you may be shackling yourself by taking it too seriously.*

Q **So what's so good about silly games?**

A *Sometimes the silliness is the creativity and becomes the rule. Probably the most well-known version of nonsensical rule-making (in the UK anyway) is a game called 'Mornington Crescent', played on the radio as part of a BBC show* I'm Sorry I Haven't A Clue. *Each panellist takes it in turn to say the name of a London train or underground station, supposedly mapping out a legitimate route across London. The (apparent) aim of the game is to convince the other panellists that your latest station is a legitimate 'move', while preventing the next player from being able to say 'Mornington Crescent'. Although many people have tried to fathom seemingly countless rules of this game, the whole thing is, in fact, improvisational nonsense that apes the ridiculous squabbling over rules that some families revel in during board games, and also satirises the cliquishness that comes from being supposedly 'in-the know' about how to play a particularly obscure game. All kinds of new rules and variations for Mornington Crescent are continually being documented and discussed on the Web. If you must, check out: www.isihac.co.uk/games/mcvariations/index.html*

6

Beanz meanz Heinz

If you want to get people excited about your ideas very quickly, there's nothing to beat a short and snappy statement of your aims and beliefs (except, perhaps, offering them money).

Many a great art movement has been established through sloganeering.

Good sloganeering is all about selling you, your idea, your work or your product in a statement that is concise, memorable and clever (or at least two of these things). Like the film business practice of pitching, the trick is to grab attention and hold people's interest for a brief period of time, leaving them always with the feeling that there is something more that lies beyond the initial rhetoric and showmanship.

Good sloganeering (and pitching) means being concise without being vacuous; distilling the essence of your work rather than reducing it to bland oversimplification. Movie posters are a good source of inspiration in this regard. They always come with a strapline or a slogan:

'Mischief. Mayhem. Soap.' (*Fight Club*, 1999)

'The general who became a slave. The slave who became a gladiator. The gladiator who defied an Emperor.' (*Gladiator*, 2000)

Here's an idea for you...

Make up the words, as well as the slogans. 'Sloganeering' itself doesn't appear in most dictionaries. Inventing words, especially by combining the meaning of two or more others, can make your slogan more noticeable. Gordon's described G&Ts made with their own branded gin as 'innervigoration'. And French Connection UK used just an anagram for their 'fcuk' (unforgettable!).

Make a list of the ones you like and the ones you loathe. Why do you feel that way about them? More often than not, the best slogans have some sort of 'one, two, three' rhythm, combining three words, phrases or sentences.

When coming up with your own slogan, don't overcomplicate and, above all, keep it short. It's easier to remember a simple phrase, especially if it's a familiar one – 'Just do it' (Nike) – or a common saying, slightly changed: 'I think, therefore IBM'. Of course, if takes a great deal of marketing spend to 'own' a phrase like 'Just do it', but there's no harm in trying. What everyday words or statements would you like to own? Make a list and stake your claim. Alternatively, use an online translation service like AltaVista's Babel Fish to mangle someone else's slogan by translating from English into a couple of other languages and then back into English. 'Just do it' via Portuguese and Greek becomes 'made simply'.

Unusual spelling, bad grammar and strange capitalisation can all draw attention to your words, but bear in mind it's easy to look cheesy: Kall Kwik, anyone? Alliteration might make more of your message. Rhyming ('Beanz meanz Heinz') or punning ('Do me a Quaver') can often be short, funny *and* clever. You might even come up with something that people will remember for centuries, like Caesar's 'Veni Vidi Vici'.

For a slogan to be effective, it needs to be seen (and read). The positioning or siting of your slogan can make all the difference. Try chalking your slogan on the wall, writing it on a post-it note, posting it on a website, projecting it on a screen or animating it on video (though *don't* try spraying it on next-door's car).

Artists have long used slogans. The surrealists were among the first to appropriate political-style activism for art with such meaningless slogans as 'Parents! Tell your children your dreams' or 'If you love love, you'll love Surrealism'. They also set down their principles, policies and intentions in a public 'Manifesto of Surrealism'.

In the early twentieth century, any artistic movement worth its paint had a manifesto. The Italian futurists, English vorticists, French Dadaists and German expressionists were all producing 'calls to revolution'. Nowadays you're more likely to find Danish film-makers doing it: Dogme 95's 'Vow of Chastity' is a set of rules to counter 'certain tendencies' in today's cinema. It hasn't changed the world, but it has grown into a new genre.

So if the revolutionary nature of the manifesto has diminished, is there any point in writing one? Well it's one way to collect together a set of slogans and aphorisms to give them a coherence and weight that they might not

Try another idea...

Once you've got yourself a few slogans or even a whole manifesto, why not test their robustness by extending them, stretching them out into a longer story or putting them in a nonsensical context? Great things can flow from this kind of extended rambling, as shown in IDEA 41, *Lie, flim-flam, embellish, elaborate.*

Defining idea...

'Never work!'
GUY DEBORD

have on their own. A good example is Bruce Mau's *Incomplete Manifesto for Growth*. And in stating publicly what your principles, policies and intentions are, you're more likely to convince others to join you and help you realise your intentions. And if you're serious about your creative work, being able to articulate at length and in detail to others about who you are and what you want to do is an essential skill.

How did it go?

Q   So what do I do with my slogan once I've got it?

A   *Ultimately, getting noticed may be more important than what you have to say. If you could get your message on the moon, for example, visible to everyone on Earth, would it matter what you actually said? Marshall McLuhan, the Canadian media theorist who coined the aphorism 'the medium is the message', once said that content 'has about as much importance as the stencilling on the casing of an atomic bomb'. For those of us in the business of content creation, clearly this statement is nonsense, but it's also clear that an understanding of the means of delivery, as well as the content, of your message is essential.*

Q   So if I don't 'sell' anything, does that mean my slogan hasn't worked?

A   *No. Sloganeering doesn't always have to be about selling something. If you haven't already, take a look (and if you have, take another look) at the work of American conceptual artist Barbara Kruger. She crusades against the control that political and commercial statements have over our hearts and minds, and through the use of slogans in such works as 'I shop, therefore I am' (1987) exposes the manipulations of the media. Her slogans are not selling anything, but they are telling us something about how we live.*

7

Restrict your choices to broaden your possibilities

It's perfectly possible to produce recipes for success based on just a few ingredients. More bread, anyone?

Every now and then, try to immerse yourself in creative exercises that use only one colour, palette, font or sound.

In other books that celebrate personal creativity, you'll probably read a lot of guff about how 'anything's possible' and there are 'no limits' to what you can do. If you work without limits, however, it's very easy to lose focus and for your projects to become sprawling, rambling efforts that require a huge amount of editing and refinement – either by you or by someone else.

Imposing just one silly rule about what you're not allowed to do can have interesting results – such as setting yourself the challenge of using only twenty-five letters of the alphabet to write with, as follows.

Here's an idea for you... **The founding father of bossa nova, Jobim, was once criticised (by an idiot) for being only concerned with rhythm and lacking any facility with tune or melody. Jobim's creative response was a tune called 'One Note Samba', a fantastic example of restriction at work. Could you dream up a song that is based around one single note?**

'You might think it silly to hamstring your output in such a way, and at first it looks impossibly hard to do – but it's still worth a go, if only to gain a bit of insight into how your writing might spiral off down tortuous paths as you try to avoid using a solitary non-consonant. Although now, as you look at this paragraph, you may think it's not that hard at all.'

We write with restrictions all the time anyway without really noticing it. (It's the letter 'e' by the way.) Every time you send someone a holiday postcard you're writing in a strict frame with a limited word count – and your writing style changes accordingly: 'Weather great. Wish you were here. Etc.'

Even if you're not on holiday, try and use postcards for all your written communications rather than A4 stationery (and think of the trees you'll save). If you're feeling really keen, try using only the back of business cards.

If you need further inspiration in this area, pick up a book on one of the greatest examples of restriction: haiku poetry. Haiku is a seventeen-syllable verse form consisting of three metrical units of five, seven and five syllables. Each haiku always includes a 'kigo', a season word, such as blossom to indicate spring, mosquitoes to indicate summer, etc.

A radical way of restricting yourself is to kill off a bit of work you're in love with – that seems to be the real heart of your project but is actually throwing everything else out of balance. Go to IDEA 15, *Bin your best work.*

Try another idea...

Restriction can be just as effective in fields other than writing, such as painting. Consider Picasso's famous blue period, or Turner's concentrated globs of orange or red. Some artists simply fall in love with one colour. Yves Klein went as far as to patent the ultramarine colour known as International Klein Blue, or IKB.

Film-maker Derek Jarman famously made a movie *Blue* that is just that – over an hour's worth of luminous blue and nothing else, accompanied by snippets of sound, music and Jarman's own voice talking about his own blindness and approaching death from AIDS-related illnesses. It is strangely affecting and effective.

Defining
idea...

'I think people who are not artists often think artists are inspired. But if you work at your art you don't have time to be inspired. Out of the work comes the work.'
JOHN CAGE, composer

Switching off a sense in this way can augment your understanding of the world around you. Try walking around the house for a while with your eyes closed (be careful!). If you want a good laugh, make a movie while you're doing it and see how the resulting footage differs from what you'd film with your eyes open. Better still, play a game of blind man's buff with a few friends and get the person with the blindfold to film the experience (maybe have a few drinks first...). The bulk of the movie you make will undoubtedly be rubbish, but you may find a few frames of brilliance that make you think about filming in a different way. Taking this to its logical conclusion, you can always blindfold your audience...

Try cooking with only, say, three ingredients (best not do this blindfold). The more conservative among you will probably plump for eggs, flour and milk to make a pancake – very smart – but the real challenge is to use three quite disparate ingredients. 'Oysters, passion fruit and lavender', we can assure you, can be made into something really delicious.

Q   **Most of my work is done at a desk in an office and my outputs are all pretty similar. What kind of restrictions are left for me to impose?**

How did it go?

A   *If you're an office worker, you probably work with a computer or word processor quite a lot. In the digital world one of the key restrictions is file size. Anyone who has sat at a computer waiting for a file to download from the internet knows the value of dealing in kilobytes rather than megabytes: it can be the different between a five second and a five minute wait. Next time you create a computer file, see how large it is and then set yourself the challenge of halving it. For example, this chapter, typed as a Microsoft Word document, panned out at about 30k. How could I cut it down to 15k? (The first step would be to type it in a different, simpler computer application or save it in a different format.) This exercise works even better with picture files, with drastic decisions to be made about colour, resolution, the size of graphic elements and so on. The picture you end up with might have very different qualities to the one you started with. And that's the whole point of restriction!*

Q   **That's all very well, but I'm interested in the thought process, not the technology. How do I restrict that?**

A   *The technology is the thought process, but if you prefer, just stick to words. That age-old skill of précis, learnt at school, is a superb restrictive art. Take something you've written and try to reduce it to half its word length. Then halve it again.*

8

The three types of objectives: easy, hard and useless

There's no harm in shooting for the moon – as long as your gun is the size of Ethiopia. How to make targets for yourself that are achievable and not just pipe dreams.

Would-be writers often talk about sitting down one day and writing 'that novel', but really that's as silly as deciding to make a Hollywood feature as your first step into film-making.

Whenever you first enter a creative field, you will almost certainly need to start small – and know your limitations. If you're a film-maker, for example, the best way into the business is with a very short film: two minutes only, or maybe ten if you have the resources and confidence. If you're that would-be writer, write an article or a short story first, not a novel – or write a poem, maybe, as its specific form and structure can act as your safety net.

Here's an idea for you...

List all the reasons (and excuses) why the thing you want to do can't really be done. Include all the lame stuff, like 'I don't have time', 'I'm scared of making a fool of myself in public'. Once you've got all that out of your system, counter every single objection and lay out cogent ways of overcoming those obstacles. If you do this early on in your project planning, it should give you confidence that you're setting off down a good path.

If you're really set on tackling a big task, always try and break it down into smaller, more manageable chunks. (Instead of holding your breath for an hour, say, hold it for sixty separate minutes.) Writers of novels, for example, often get started by writing just one self-contained fragment or chapter that is publishable as a stand-alone short story well before the novel has been completed. By adopting this approach, the bigger project is still trundling along, but there are clear and measurable staging posts along the way to remind you that you are making genuine progress.

By busting your big project apart, you may actually discover that it is two or three different projects in disguise. We discovered this ourselves once when working on a very large and unwieldy idea for a complex online interactive game called XmasPresent. In order to get a grip on what was a rather hazy concept, we decided to tackle three basic issues one by one:

1. the basic rules of gameplay

2. the gameworld in which everything takes place

3. player interaction and communication

Over the next couple of years, all three sections spun off into separate and distinct projects, with the gameworld actually becoming a map of a fictional corporation (that became our actual business – see www.xpt.com), and the player interaction project strangely morphing into a webcam and email drama called Online Caroline (www.onlinecaroline.com). Our seemingly impossible task of building a broadband multiplayer game from scratch turned into the highly achievable and commercially successful task of producing an online drama. Meanwhile, we still managed to work out key elements of the bigger plan – so the impossible task isn't quite so impossible for us now.

Like anyone creative, we like to stretch ourselves and try new things. But we don't like the idea that all our endeavours may end in failure, or that we won't deliver all the great stuff that we know is inside our heads. One way around this is to make a list of the key elements (the design of a character, the rules of a game, the pattern on a fabric, the technical requirements of a home or garden design project) and then work on just a couple of them in complete isolation from everything else. By picking out a few readily achievable tasks, you're giving yourself some 'easy wins' that will boost your confidence and make you feel like you're progressing. This will strengthen your resolve and extend your reach when it comes to tackling those tougher tasks you know are coming down the line.

Set out your objectives in accordance with IDEA 4, *Be organised*, to ensure you use your time effectively and really get things done.

Try another idea...

'Try? There is no try. There is only do or not do.'
YODA, Jedi warrior

Defining idea...

The business guru Pete Drucker has a neat acronym for helping you understand the opportunities and dangers of any objectives you set yourself, whether big or small. He asks you to think S.M.A.R.T. by tackling these key issues every time you start a new piece of work:

Specific: do I understand exactly what the task entails?

Measurable: what constitutes success or failure or 'good value'?

Achievable: can this be done at all? What are the obvious barriers?

Realistic: can I do this with the resources I have and is it worth doing at all?

Time-related: how much time will I spend on this?

Although we're not here to encourage negative thinking, it can be a really good idea to concentrate on the achievability of your task first of all.

Q   **Setting out my objectives in a clear-headed, sensible way rather took all the fun out of what I wanted to do. Is that what you wanted?**

How did it go?

A   *Do remember that there's always room for passionate idealism and sheer strength of will in your calculations. Sometimes you just want to do something for the sake of it. People still climb mountains simply 'because they're there', and by doing so inspire us all with the power of the human spirit. Continue to set yourself a few targets that are useless, pointless or just plain mad. That way, you'll keep some of the excitement and danger that creativity should be about. You'll also take yourself beyond what you consciously know about yourself and your ideas, and that way lies new fertile areas of creativity. Just remember to allow yourself some simple, straightforward tasks occasionally and then perhaps give yourself a (wacky) reward for completing them successfully. Then even the dull stuff can still create some spark in your creative life.*

Q   **I know what my objectives are, but I *really* don't have time to devote to them now, and no, this isn't just a 'lame excuse'...So how can I make time?**

A   *Productivity guru David Allen reckons that any system you devise for 'Getting Things Done' needs to cater for every aspect of your life, not just those things you consider 'work'. Maybe you need to set some objectives and organise your home life better in order to free up more time for your creative endeavours.*

9

Make more mistakes faster

Working at speed with a high level of error can help you 'fail better'. Which means you'll get to something good quicker.

Creativity is often about speed of throughput. Believe it or not, making a hash of it at high speed may be the key to getting to where you want to go.

This idea is often attributed to Andy Grove of Intel, the processor manufacturing company that helped revolutionise the computer industry in the 1980s and 1990s. When your business is about crashing out millions of bits of finely etched silicon, it's easy to see why you might be prepared to keep the production line rolling even if a few batches get screwed up along the way.

For the sculptor who spends six months working one piece in stone, it may be less easy to write the resulting work off as a failure and start again. Nevertheless, for most of us, Grove's principle is a sound one. You have to keep scribbling and sketching, modelling and planning and thinking, setting things up to knock them down, scrumpling up bits of paper and throwing them in the bin, crashing and

Here's an idea for you...

This week, try and fire off at least a dozen ideas. In many cases, the first eleven ideas will be crap (so try to think of the twelfth one first to save time!). Don't see that as a waste of effort – see it more as a range-finder. Only by working through your early shortcomings will you hope to refine your processes on the fly – and your instincts.

rebooting your computer, working continuously with enthusiasm and energy and wit, and above all without any embarrassment about the obvious cock-ups along the way. If you do this intelligently and energetically, other people will almost certainly be affected by your positive spirit and join you on your journey. Those who write you off as foolish and annoying – well, maybe hanging out with them is just another mistake and it's time to move on.

Also remember that mistakes are not always mistakes. Look at them another way and they become happy accidents. According to movie director Robert Altman, 'Chance is another name that we give to our mistakes. And all of the best things in my films are mistakes.' Mistakes, he is saying, are the stuff of life. And for him, they are also the stuff of art. (And according to chaos theory, they are also the stuff of stuff.)

This is the same attitude to life that Oscar Wilde describes when he writes: 'Nowadays most people die of a sort of creeping common sense, and discover when it is too late that the only things one never regrets are one's mistakes.'

Defining idea...

'A life spent in making mistakes is not only more honourable but more useful than a life spent doing nothing.'
GEORGE BERNARD SHAW

Probably the most famous blunderer of them all is Alexander Fleming. Not only did he discover penicillin by accidentally contaminating some Petri dish samples and then not bothering to wash them up for a few days, he also discovered lysozyme when he didn't bother using a handkerchief and his nose accidentally dripped into a dish of bacteria. Are you creative enough not to wipe your nose for a week just to see what accidents might happen?

If you're anxious about making mistakes, try a little creative risk assessment instead. We'll show you how in IDEA 12, *Take risks.*

Try another idea...

The true moral of this story might be: if it ain't fixed, break it.

Certainly, one of the best ways to understand how some things work is to break them apart. For your family's sake, it's probably best if you work out how to put them back together again as well, although this isn't critical (unless it's grandma's Zimmer frame). And if it turns out that you've broken something irretrievably, try and find a new use for what you've got left. Look at kids: they rarely throw old broken toys away, but remodel, fuse and repurpose them for use in another game.

And talking of small kids, it's as well to remember that we only ever learn to walk after a lot of falling over. In fact, if you want to get technical about it, walking *is* falling over. If you don't believe us, get up now and lean forward like you are going to fall – then stick your leg out at the last minute. Almost inevitably, your other leg will kick in and you'll take not one step but two in order to break your fall.

So now you see that even something as basic as walking is really just a controlled way for your body to blunder around the place.

'If I had my life to live over I'd dare to make more mistakes next time.'
NADINE STAIR, poet

Defining idea...

How did it go? **Q**   **If I make mistakes at work, won't I get fired?**

A   *Actually, many forward-looking corporations do tolerate failure to some extent. At Pepsico, it is said, they used to allow executives to get away with two major screw-ups and still get promoted, in an effort to 'blood' the management team and encourage risk taking. The main point we're making here is that you can only get the blame for things that go wrong if you bother to take responsibility in the first place. Doing nothing is often the safest option in a creative life – but it's often the most stultifying too. We could give examples, but won't.*

Q   **I find making mistakes depressing, even fatiguing. Shouldn't I be feeling inspiration, rather than desperation?**

A   *If you feel yourself flagging, or getting too hung up on getting one thing right, remind yourself that if you only work through two ideas this week, you may never get to the point of rewards and satisfaction that you're after.*

10

Smash it up

Want to try a new angle on being creative? Take a break.

Have you noticed how much creativity these days has nothing at all to do with handling and manipulating physical objects?

Instead we play with ideas and concepts, we build 'creative economies' and use computers to develop 'virtual presences'. Our money is in bits and bytes, our music is downloaded with no casing, no sleeve, no CD. Digital cameras allow us to snap, edit or trash without getting a single image developed.

And yet a lot of the language of digital creativity refers to quite violent physical processes. We rip and burn music. We hit websites and trash files. So, just for a change, we want you to get physical and spend some time enjoying the tactile quality of working with physical objects.

Some artists perform acts of violence on more unusual objects. Consider Damien Hirst's treatment of sheep and cows, or Grayson Perry's 'defacing' of his pots. This is more breaking down barriers with their past than breaking new ground. Consider the play of young children, or young animals in the zoo (or in the wild, but don't get too close). Their play involves an inordinate amount of smashing and bashing (and biting and chewing, but that's another story), and out of all this physical exertion creative thought processes emerge.

Here's an
idea for
you...

Pick up something within easy reach right now – a coffee cup, a phone, whatever – and spend five minutes (at least!) manipulating it. Explore its surface with your fingers, feel its texture and enjoy its weight. Now start getting under its skin. Scratch it. Knock it about a bit. Or drop it from a height. Onto a hard surface. If you've broken it, pick up the pieces. Are there sharp fragments with a different texture? Do the dents and bumps reflect light in an interesting way? Now you can begin to see how smashing things up can change the way you perceive things and your creative train of thought.

Indeed, to divorce creativity from the business of making and manipulating is very often pretty bogus. People who tell you that you can create intellectual capital or a 'knowledge economy' without any form of manufacturing base or physical resource are probably kidding themselves. (Here ends the political broadcast…)

If you really don't like the idea of screwing around with real objects, there's a great website at www.sodaplay.com/constructor/index.htm which allows you to construct and play with a mind-boggling array of virtual objects that can adopt amazing physical behaviours.

If nothing else, by keeping your hands busy, you can allow your brain to wander. In a way, what we're talking about here is an advanced form of thumb twiddling (extreme perhaps, in Damien Hirst's case, but twiddling nevertheless).

Concentrating on the physical properties of the world around you is also – curiously – a very ancient and traditional way of connecting with your spiritual side (if you have one). It's not a coincidence that most religions adopt a series of physical rituals as part of the act of worship.

If you like these ideas for smashing things up, take a look at what we've got to say about hammers in IDEA 20, *Pick the wrong tools for the job.*

Try another idea...

An obvious one is the Christian tradition of re-enacting the last supper with the taking of bread and wine as an act of communion. A more bizarre and arresting example is the voodoo tradition of building shrines to the dead using materials such as dolls heads squashed into jars, bundles of cigars, bird feathers and much, much more.

Indeed, building your own personal shrine of treasured objects can be extremely useful for revealing aspects of your own personality and your creative interests that you may not have noticed before. If you're particularly drawn to this kind of activity, have a go at making your own voodoo doll of someone you don't like and stick a few pins in it. See for yourself just how superstitious this makes you feel. And explore the niggling doubt that maybe – just maybe – there's a connection between your physical torture of the doll and the fate of the person the doll is representing.

'Every act of creation is first of all an act of destruction.'
PABLO PICASSO

Defining idea...

How did it go?

Q   **This kind of exercise isn't really going to help me when it comes to the day-to-day business of making computer presentations and producing word-processed documents, now is it?!**

A   *Actually, it's quite interesting to think about how you could 'smash up' a computer presentation. Could you perhaps look at ways of degrading or defacing the screen, blurring images, stretching fonts or adding graffiti? Or perhaps you could shuffle the pages on your screen like a pack of cards and 'deal' them in a random order?*

Q   **So isn't this only really relevant for computer-based projects?**

A   *No, not at all. In fact, you may want to try blurring the boundaries of the physical and virtual 'smashing up' by planning your presentation using a physical object rather than working inside the software application itself. The most obvious physical implement would be a pen, but that'd be boring. How about planning your next presentation using only a ball of Blu-tack? (We actually managed to do this once, to deliver a presentation about Russian leaders of the twentieth century...)*

11

Look at things another way

Changing your point of view rearranges your physical relationship with everything around you. And brings a whole new meaning to 'hanging around' at parties.

It can also force conceptual changes —
like thinking about a door as a 'portal' instead
of just a door. Or thinking of it as 'a jar'.
Or even imagining yourself being the door.

You've probably already been told several times to 'consider the bigger picture'. But how do you get yourself into a position to do it?

The next time you want to get a better handle on a situation, try and inspect it from on high: either literally, by standing on a chair or climbing a ladder (best not to do this in meetings too often), or metaphorically by imagining yourself looking from very far away at all the things that are currently up close and personal. This will help you gain some mental and emotional distance from the things and people you work with, and help you think more clearly about the possibilities open to you.

Here's an idea for you... **Another obvious way to change your perspective is to 'rescale'. Imagine big things as small, and vice versa. For example, take a big thing and treat it like a little thing (like a new Lamborghini).**

Changing your point of view needn't always be about looking – you can use your other senses too. Instead of concentrating on what things look like, make a note about how they feel (rough, smooth, warm, cold, soft, hard) or smell.

Here's an exercise you can try in the privacy of your own desk. Take a relatively small object, such as a cup, stapler or bulldog clip. Now subject your object to a series of experiments that will force you to look at things in a different way. Keep a notebook handy and write down all the thoughts that occur to you.

First, turn your object upside down (if you picked a full coffee cup, that's your look-out). Think about how its shape has changed, how it might look like something else, how its function may be impaired by being upside down, how it might become useful as something other than what it is.

Draw it roughly with your non-drawing hand so that you have a deliberately naïve and scruffy sketch. What does it look like now?

Now put it outside and look at it through a window, so that it looks abandoned or 'not yours'. Does it look comfortable outside? Does it look like it belongs there? If not, why not? If you can bear it, leave the object outside for a few days and see how it weathers. Does it change colour? Does mould or rust form? If you can't bear it, pluck up courage to abandon it in a public place for 20 minutes anyway and write down how you feel about its potential loss.

Now bring it back indoors. Put it behind you and look at it through a mirror. What you're looking at now is its reverse image. Reach out and try and touch that image. How do you feel, being able to look but not touch? Shine a torch on it and see how light and shadow play upon it, both directly and via the mirror image. What shadow shapes can you create?

Children are exceptionally good at improvising with objects and using them in ways they weren't designed to be used. Remember what it was like to play like that by going to IDEA 25, *Be childlike*.

Try another idea...

Now it's time to abuse your object a bit. Put it on a turntable and watch it spin around; put it under water; or suspend it on a wire and swing it. Feel free to play with it like a cat plays with a mouse. Don't be afraid to break it. And when you're done, hide it in a place where you think no one will ever find it (like a dog with a bone).

If you're enjoying this relationship with your object, take it further. Give it a name, or write a caption or slogan to go with it. Wrap it up and give it to someone as a special present. Photograph it as if it were a supermodel. Write a song about it. Wear it. Cook it. Probably best not to eat it.

The important thing is always to challenge yourself about how you perceive the object, how you use and abuse it, and what it could potentially become given your changed perspective.

'Cinema, radio, television, magazines are a school of inattention: people look without seeing, listen in without hearing.'
ROBERT BRESSON, French film director

Defining idea...

49

How did it go?

Q **These exercises are too silly and time consuming for a busy person like me. What's a more sensible and practical way of looking at a bigger picture?**

A *If you want a bigger picture of the world but don't have the time or inclination to explore it by yourself, get an atlas or map. Maps are powerful ways of manipulating people's perception of the world. Mapmakers tend to put their own country right smack bang in the centre of the map – despite the fact that in depicting a globe, you can basically put any part of the world you like at the centre. A simple way of reframing your own position in the world might be to draw a map with you at the centre of it.*

Q **How is all this messing about with coffee cups and the like going to help me 'think different', then?**

A *By forcing yourself to act differently in relation to objects (or ideas) and to look at them differently, it's as though you're trying to change the person who is doing the looking. We all have different aspects to our personalities: dreamer, realist, critic, etc. Imagine these as different people, all standing around looking at whatever you are looking at, with the same person coming to dominate in a particular situation. Now imagine they are looking at the same thing, but this time through a telescope, so that only one can look at a time. Is there someone whose point of view usually gets ignored? How about giving them the telescope for the day and getting everyone else to shut up for a bit?*

12

Take risks

Just what are you prepared to put on the line in order to be more creative?

Taking risks can radically change the way you live.

We all have very different ideas about what risk actually is. For some, the potential embarrassment of singing in public is just too risky. For others, climbing a mountain with the possibility of losing a limb or even dying comes under the heading 'fun'.

In the field of creativity, it's unusual to find people willing to risk death or serious injury for their work – but they are out there. Magician and showman David Blaine, for example, incarcerated himself in a glass box with no food for forty days. Performance artist Chris Burden crucified himself on the bonnet of a car. William Burroughs wrote many of his most famous works, such as *The Naked Lunch*, while under the influence of powerful drugs.

Quite often artists work with the deliberate intent of confronting social taboos. Damien Hirst and his fellow 'Britartists' definitely succeeded in 'shocking the nation' in the 1990s by using animal carcasses and pseudo-pornographic images to grab our attention. Around the same time, musician and artist Bill Drummond set fire to a million pounds in cash – deliberately wasting the money. And Michael Landy went one step further, using an industrial shredder to destroy *all* his possessions.

Here's an idea for you... **Draw a square grid. Mark the left-hand side as 'Safe', the right as 'Dangerous', the bottom as 'Serious' and the top as 'Silly'. Now position your creative ideas on the grid by marking a dot with your pencil. Serious and safe ideas live somewhere in the bottom left corner. What would you have to do to them to push them into other areas?**

We're not suggesting that you try anything like this (hmm, well maybe…), but you do need to ask yourself where you draw the line. For example, how politically active do you want to be in terms of your creativity? Throughout history, artists, writers and musicians have been thrown into prison or executed because their ideas were considered anti-social and subversive. Alexander Solzhenitsyn, for example, was exiled to Siberia for many years because of his writings. On the other hand, Ezra Pound flirted dangerously with Fascist politics, tarnishing his reputation as a poet and critic, and instead of prison was carted off to a mental institution.

How conservative or radical you want to be with your ideas is very much a personal decision, but you do need to understand the scale by which you can measure those ideas. For example, think back to moments in your life when you have felt deeply embarrassed or exposed in public. What caused them, and how did you react to each situation? Did you deliberately put yourself in a risky situation or were you ambushed? Did you do something to retrieve the situation, or did you simply get angry – or run away? By looking back over these events, you should be able to get a closer reading of what your personal fears and inhibitions are. In many ways, you may well have already been very creative in managing to ignore or suppress them.

But you should also think of developing creative ideas that confront and expose your fears. At the most basic level, if you have a fear of heights, make yourself go to a very high place. If you don't like snakes, go to the zoo and spend an hour in the reptile house. Write down how you feel, dramatise it, tell people about it in such a way that they feel the 'buzz' you felt at the time.

Another important question regarding your 'risk assessment' is: what have you got to lose? Make an inventory of all the things in your life that you value, that define who you are, that make you happy – family, friends, home comforts, holidays, etc. Now score the importance of each out of ten. Take your time: these are important to you.

Now, take all the things that have scored eight or less, and think of an action or a situation that would put each one in jeopardy. In fact, take each as the subject matter for your next creative project and see how you would cope with losing them – or at least exposing your own dependency on them in public. For example, how would you cope if you lost your house or flat because you failed to meet the mortgage payments or pay the rent; burnt it down; got kicked out by your partner; got hounded out by the community…

Follow through the consequences of some of these – what kind of creative work would lead to not paying the rent or falling out with your partner or being offered a new job?

When we take risks, we often talk of the dangers of 'exposing oneself'. Now, we're not recommending streaking as a creative activity, but there's a lot to be said for doing something silly in public in order to get a laugh, and generally shrugging off one's inhibitions, as IDEA 22, *All time is playtime*, shows.

Try another idea...

'It is not because things are difficult that we do not dare; it is because we do not dare that they are difficult.'
SENECA

Defining idea...

53

Even if you don't take this line of thinking any further, you should now be more aware of what kind of creative risks you really are prepared to take. And what risks you're actively choosing to avoid.

How did it go?

Q   I want to push myself, but I don't want to upset people. How should I go about it?

A   *To take a risk, you need to have something at stake. As a general rule, you shouldn't really gamble with other people's chips. But there are moments when your creative decisions are bound to have consequences for the people around you. One way to rethink this dilemma is not to worry about what you might lose or who you might offend, but put all that creative energy into finding innovative ways of not losing. For example, it's an old rock star cliché to throw a TV out of the hotel window while on tour, but what if you could work out how to do so without it breaking? Questioning the risks in this positive way doesn't have to stop you doing anything – it just makes you do it in a different way.*

Q   It's easy to talk about taking risks when you don't have responsibilities. What if you do?

A   *It's easy to come up with reasons for not taking risks, especially those compelling reasons, like a job, mortgage or family. Sometimes the biggest risk, though, is that you'll feel unfulfilled until you do. Talk to the people who share your responsibilities and to whom you are responsible. Unless what you are proposing is completely foolhardy and not a calculated risk, chances are they'll support you.*

13

Being unfashionable

There are pros and cons to going in the opposite direction to everyone else. Not least the constant need to avoid getting trampled.

Have you noticed how anyone who very publicly and successfully rejects or upsets the status quo can very quickly become deeply, deeply fashionable?

The music industry is particularly good at finding artists who initially shock – Madonna, Eminem, Slipknot – but then become very much part of the mainstream. In a sense, the quickest way to become fashionable is to reject fashion: to disparage current trends, and occupy spaces and positions that no one else wants to inhabit.

You probably have an image of those who reject fashion in this way: highly original thinkers – eccentric even – living in a part of town that's 'bohemian' and 'cool', dressing in odd clothes and breaking social taboos by saying the unsayable, thinking the unthinkable. But expending too much creative energy on deliberately being *un*fashionable in this way can make you as much of a slave to your times as anyone else.

Here's an idea for you... **Take up a new activity – like golf or train-spotting, something you would normally consider 'deeply uncool' – and do it *ironically*. Persuade a few friends to give it a go too. See how long it takes before the irony lifts and you start enjoying it for what it is.**

To our mind, there are five very different types who reject or ignore fashion in various ways:

1. THE SHOW-OFF

If you define yourself by your opposition to the mainstream, you're not necessarily being true to yourself. Knee-jerk anti-fashionistas abound in the creative industries. Their kind of opposition is not original and doesn't automatically produce good or 'authentic' work. In the end, it's just another form of publicity seeking.

2. THE ECCENTRIC

Some people are just naturally odd and therefore beyond fashion. Think of Leigh Bowery, in his weird and wonderful get-ups, Grayson Perry, Turner Prize-winning potter, who spends half his life dressed up in baby-doll dresses, or Vivian Stanshall of the Bonzo Dog Doo Dah Band. What makes these people distinctive is that they manage to be original without being deliberately or knowingly perverse. No-one can teach you how to be like this. You've either got it or you haven't.

3. THE GOLFER

There are some people who really are completely oblivious to fashion – or perhaps the word's impervious. They will often tell you they 'know what they like', and we should admire them for that. But this kind of firm-mindedness can also lead to creative stagnation. Think of middle-aged men who've stopped caring about what they wear, who listen to the same old music and perhaps have developed a particular hobby such as wine-making, stamp collecting or golf (*the* sport for people who know nothing about fashion). We're not saying this is a bad way to live, by the way (Rob loves golf and Tim makes wine); it's just not the best way to remain open to creative possibilities.

4. THE EXCLUDED

Before we start sounding snooty here, remember that the vast majority of people in this world simply can't afford to be fashionable. When there's poor education, poor housing and unemployment to worry about, you don't really have the time or the inclination to worry about the latest trends. Having said that, there is such a thing as 'poverty chic', and it's not unknown for struggling artists to move into the poorer areas of a town or city, dress in charity shop clothing, take over derelict warehouse spaces and turn them into studios, or convert shoddy clubs and shops into 'cool' clubs and eateries. In London, both Hoxton and Hackney are prime examples of poverty chic.

You can only tap into the spirit of the times if you put yourself about a bit. See how in IDEA 34, *Network near, network far.*

Try another idea...

Defining
idea...

'Anyone can look for fashion in a boutique or history in a museum. The creative person looks for history in a hardware store and fashion in an airport.'
ROBERT WIEDER, US journalist

If you've the time, explore farther afield in your town of choice and see if you can second guess where the next 'Hoxton' will be, the next unfashionable area that people will occupy and subsequently make fashionable. (In London, our money is on either New Cross or Muswell Hill, by the way.)

5. THE *ZEITGEIST* CHASER

You'll have noticed by now that we're pretty down on the idea that fashion is actually important to the creative individual. The notion of catching the spirit of the times (which is what *Zeitgeist* means in German), though, is important. Fashion is to a large extent an industrial term and not something the creative individual should be too fussed about. It's manufactured and manipulated, it's 'set' and happens in 'seasons'. Fashion is the corporate monster that sells everyone the same hat with the slogan 'be different' on it.

Zeitgeist, on the other hand, is in the air and of the moment. To catch it requires less planning and strategy and more spontaneity. But if you develop a nose for it, it can be a very powerful part of your work.

Q   So what can I actually do to capture the *Zeitgeist*?

A   We're not sure we can give you any great tips about how to develop that nose, other than keep those nostrils flared by being alert and natural. If it's at all about clothes, it's about that moment when you for no reason at all decide to buy that silly hat (a Kangol) or those naff shoes (Hush Puppies) and then discover that, six months later, everyone's wearing them. It's about having crushes on colours or typefaces without worrying whether anyone else likes them. It's about being drawn instinctively into unpopulated or uncharted areas, not because you want to be seen by others standing alone, but because you find that place creatively stimulating right now.

Q   But isn't chasing the *Zeitgeist* still a bit desperate?

A   Sure, there's what is known as 'the Zeitgeist industry' full of people trying desperately to be ahead of the curve. But essentially they are an extension of the fashion industry, staking out claims to future markets. What you need to concentrate on is discovering how the things that made you a creative individual on the inside can map onto the outside world. As always, you have to be clear in your creative work about when you are really following your own muse (or is that your nose?), and when you're actually being directed and shaped by the needs and desires of the marketplace.

How did it go?

59

14

Never make a sequel (unless you can make several)

If you've produced something successful, you have a decision to make. Should you repeat the trick again with the same successful results or challenge yourself to try something completely different?

If one piece of work is great, then two pieces must be greater...right?

We all know that attempts to capitalise on success are not always a good idea. For a start, nobody likes to be seen as a one-trick pony. It makes you sound like you never progress; that you're not testing yourself, not developing your talents. On the other hand, if you keep flitting about from idea to idea, there's a danger that you could become quite good at a lot of things (a polymath, even!) but that you'll never stick at one thing long enough to become an acknowledged master.

Here's an idea for you...

One game to play is with the title of your sequel. Rather than sticking a 2 on the end, can you come up with something witty and eye-catching? (Think *Aliens*, *Die Harder*, *Honey I Blew Up the Kids* and *Apocalypse Later* – OK, we made that last one up.) Sounds really silly, doesn't it? In most cases when you play this game, you'll get that uneasy feeling of spreading yourself very, very thin. But if you don't – then maybe that sequel is on after all!

Generally it is true that you don't advance your creative credit very much by doing one good thing over and over again. It is, though, a really good way to improve your bank balance and generally make a living. (And let's face it – most people's working lives are precisely about carrying out the same processes and performances day after day.) To take the obvious example of the movie business, nobody would make any great artistic claim for, say, *Speed 2* or *Predator 2*, but it's highly likely nevertheless that they made their money back in spades.

But before you think we're being too curmudgeonly about sequels and start yelling '*Godfather 2*, you fools' or '*Toy Story 2*, eejits!', let's just assert quickly that there's nothing wrong with sequels if the spur for making them is an interest in delving deeper into the sequences and situations that produced great work in the first place. A lot of great writers, for example, are instinctively drawn to particular types of character and situation. In the case of crime writers, a whole series of novels can really help to develop a story world and a fully rounded and endlessly entertaining main character such as Sherlock Holmes or Inspector Morse.

In most cases where a follow-up is worth doing, you may well find that one sequel is not enough. You may have dug enough material up for a complete and coherent cycle of works – or a full-blow franchise, such as Harry Potter or *The Simpsons*. One might even suggest that a follow-up 'number two' work (there's a cheap joke in there somewhere) is only worth bothering with if you've already developed the creative confidence to think about making numbers three, four, five, six and seven (*à la* J.K. Rowling).

A good test to try out, should you find yourself in a situation where a sequel seems appealing, is to plan out on paper not just one but seven new versions of your original concept, or a series of seven new episodes/iterations. Perhaps with each iteration you could add new features, just as mobile phone manufacturers keep adding more and more functions with each successive model. Another alternative would be to go the Swiss army knife route, and find ways of squeezing in new tools into your basic design. Or you could remodel your ideas for different markets: a widget for men, one for women, one for kids, one for sporty people, one for older people, etc. If you have a taste for the surreal, take a moment to think about launching your best ideas with new 'flavours' – what would a minty version be like, or a lemon sherbert version?

Remember too that sequels aren't always made by the same people who created the original version. It may be that by handing over control of a creative project to someone else, you can free yourself up for new work – and another person's handling of your old ideas might actually breathe new life into the project.

Sometimes it just isn't possible to repeat good tricks because the technology you've been using has become outmoded. Get around this problem with IDEA 46, *Tools of the trade – technology*.

Try another idea...

'*This World is not Conclusion. A Sequel stands beyond – Invisible, as Music – But positive, as Sound.*'
EMILY DICKINSON

Defining idea...

63

Q   You are joking right? I don't have enough ideas for a sequel so why should I do one?

A   *Then are you sure you have enough ideas for the first one? Or might you be stretching it a bit thin? A friend of ours once sent a manuscript to a publisher of romantic novels to be told that the publisher loved it, but wouldn't consider it unless there was enough material for a fistful of follow-ups – to be sure the characters had complete lives in them.*

Q   How do I absolutely know when the time is right to do a follow-up?

A   *Well, usually someone with a business head is probably already knocking on your door because of the success of your initial idea. Remember, this kind of thing is a business decision as well as a creative decision – and may involve several other people. This may sound odd, but perhaps the first thing to think about is what kind of holidays you like to go on. Are you the kind of person who goes back to the same place each summer, or do you prefer to move on each year and sample another part of the world? Now think about going back to a place where you had a really great time. How much of the experience would you repeat and what things would you do differently? When you revisit ideas with the intention of revamping or reapplying them, take a tour around them like you're a returning tourist and determine precisely which bits you have come back for.*

15

Bin your best work

Identifying the key components of a creative product may not be as obvious as you think. Sometimes it pays to take out the best bit and see what's left.

Yes, you heard us right. Leave the bathwater, throw out the baby — and let the one underneath come up for air.

You've probably spent hours going through a piece of creative work that doesn't quite hang together, wondering what the weak element is so that you can expunge it. But quite often, it's the ideas and sequences that you're deeply in love with – the bits that seem to 'work' for you – that are throwing everything else out of balance. So be brave, take a deep breath and rub out the absolutely best thing about your work: then see how everything else stands up. You might be surprised by how even and harmonious the resulting elements are (or you could be stabbing yourself in the head with a fork, saying 'Why, why, why?').

Curiously, you might even find that when you take something seemingly significant out, the ideas and themes that were represented in those best bits are in fact still present in the work – you just hadn't noticed them. Script editors have a brutal way

Here's an idea for you... **Edit your photo collection by taking out all the best photos: those that are well taken, well framed or have a strong emotional significance for you. Now organise everything that's left into one single sequence. You should find that your collection has a much more homogeneous look and feel. It may even represent a slightly more powerful pictorial record of your life, since you are now seeing it in a clearer version.**

of talking about this process, referring to it as 'killing your babies'; that is, accepting that some of the great ideas on which the project seemed to depend at first will now have to die in order to rescue the piece as a whole.

In films, it's not uncommon for a 'big scene' to end up on a cutting room floor – a scene where some key action takes place or a revelation is made, such as a character finally getting to say something that had been suppressed until that point. These moments very often appear overblown in the context of the movie as a whole. Take them out and the rest of the movie all of a sudden becomes more subtle, with its references to something you never get to see or which the characters never quite get to say.

Walter Murch, the famous editor of such films as *The Conversation*, *The Godfather* and *Apocalypse Now*, has a 'blue light' theory, which is his analogy for the need to take away a key element of a scene. His example involves lighting a particular scene using a blue light because 'blueness' is going to be important to the atmosphere of a particular scene. But that once switched on, this blue bulb, the source of all 'blueness' in the room tends to dominate: it's too blue. So you unscrew the bulb and open your eyes to other sources of blue, things that are more 'authentically blue' and that interact with other colours in more interesting ways. 'You wind up taking out the very thing that you thought was the sole source of an idea. And when you take it out, you see that not only is the idea still present, it's more organically related to everything else'.

If your family will bear it, you can try this discipline with your meals too. Make an apple pie without any apple in it. Cook a Sunday roast chicken with all the trimmings – but without the chicken! Suddenly the potatoes, the gravy, the veggies will take up more of everyone's attention. The whole flavour and atmosphere of the meal will be different. And yet the chicken will still be there in spirit. It's a Zen thing...

Or even try it with your family. Assemble all the members together – then nip off down the pub.

One way to remove your best bits is to build up an idea around a central core (maybe a sound loop that you then work up into a song). Then you start to remove pieces one by one to see whether the piece can still stand up – much as in IDEA 43, *Play creative Jenga*.

Try another idea...

'*Try any goddam thing you like, no matter how boringly normal or outrageous. If it works, fine. If it doesn't, toss it. Toss it even if you love it.*'
STEPHEN KING

Defining idea...

How did it go? **Q I'm finding it hard to be objective about my own work, so I can't really identify which 'babies' I should be killing. Any thoughts re *modus operandi*?**

A *A lot of our work we do together. This means we can kill each other's babies. Seriously, all creative people need an editor at some point – someone else who will be honest with you about what they think, who has their own very clear creative agenda (preferably one that you admire) and who you trust to take a hatchet to your work. A good example would be Ezra Pound's relationship with T.S. Eliot during the writing of the famous poem* The Wasteland. *Originally, Eliot's poem was a lot longer and a lot less 'modernist'. Pound had no compunction in drawing a line through great chunks of Eliot's work – writing that you or I would consider great work. He also added notes and his own creative suggestions. Basically, he Pounded it into shape. Ultimately this ruthless editing was necessary in order to produce a masterpiece. If you haven't met someone like this yet, add it to your to-do list.*

Q If I cut out my best bits of creative work, I'll have nothing left. How will that help?

A *Well, that could happen sometimes. What it means is that you may need to start afresh with something completely different. Remember, nothing is lost forever. If you keep all your off-cuts and deletions, you can come back to them another day when you can meet them more as strangers.*

16

Seek out criticism

How do you get people to tell you bad things about yourself and your work – without it being too humiliating or hurtful?

One of the main problems about criticism is that it's all too often seen as a negative thing. But constructive criticism isn't just about picking holes in other people's buildings.

It's perfectly possible – nay, essential – for your chosen critics to talk about the positive aspects of your work, and to tell you what you're good at. In fact, we insist that you always ask people first to tell you what they actually like about what you do before allowing them to put the boot in about the things they don't like.

Sadly, the plain truth is that it's always much easier to get bad criticism than good, which is particularly irksome if, like many people, you don't really know what is good yourself. People just have a natural tendency to be negative about new ideas, and many a badly managed brainstorming session has failed to nurture innovative thinking because everyone concerned has killed off all the great ideas before they have had time to take shape and become robust.

Here's an idea for you...

Working in a team makes it easier to give and take criticism, because everyone is working for a common cause. Out of this open atmosphere, critical slang or shorthand can develop. If you work in a team, try to consciously develop this in your own group. In our collaboration, we have a number of catchphrases that help us move swiftly though common points of criticism. For example, if one of us attempts to over-egg something to ram home a point, the other will say 'Viking helmet' (referring to a time when Tim mistakenly thought that having characters wear a Viking helmet in a scene would somehow make it funnier).

To defend yourself against this general state of affairs, never ask a neutral and woolly 'so what do you think?' kind of question of anyone. Encourage your chosen critic to be positive and give them direction with something like: 'What bits did you enjoy?' or 'What did I get right, then?' Even then, you may find it hard to get a straight answer. The curious thing about humans is that very often they'll start off being hyper-polite and rather shallow about the things they like, but only really come to life and get specific about what's wrong with your work.

Don't accept an 'it's very nice, dear' either (never get your mum to be your critic, by the way – you went through all that as a kid and she's just too damned good at it!). Even worse, you must shun the kind of knee-jerk 'I love it' you sometimes get from friends who are trying to be kind and supportive. Again, get specific. Ask them: 'What do you think of this bit?' Without waiting to be asked, explain to them some of the thinking behind your work so they have something to think about and react to.

Do not accept wholesale assassination of you and your ideas from anyone. They can say that something is not working or could be improved – that's constructive – but do not allow them to assert that the work is a waste of time and thus imply that you are no good at what you do – that's destructive. For example, the worst sin to commit in a comedy writing workshop is to say that someone's work is 'not funny'. If a joke is 'not funny' it means that it's not really a joke at all. If the writer is 'not funny', it means they're not really a comedian and should be doing something else for a living, like undertaking. To say, rather, that a joke could be improved still gives the joke teller hope and a reason to carry on. The aim with all good criticism is not to kill off creativity, just to kill off bad technique.

Make sure you move in a wide enough circle of friends to draw on the right people in times of need. See how to do this in IDEA 34, *Network near, network far.* *Try another idea...*

This is a particularly sensitive point when your project or ideas are in an early stage of development and very fragile. Too much tough love or an insensitive comment can be fatal.

You need different kinds of critics at different stages of your creative development. For example, people with no experience and no understanding of your process probably aren't that useful to you until you reach the nether regions of your project and you have an end product that requires evaluation.

'Can you tell what it is yet?'
ROLF HARRIS

Defining idea...

How did
it go?

Q   I'm not sure what to do with the feedback I've received from people. Any useful suggestions?

A   *You should always note down what people say about your work so you can reflect upon it at a later date. In some cases it can be helpful to get written feedback from people, rather than relying on the spoken word or a casual conversation. Getting your critics to write you a note or an email perhaps a day after your initial encounter can be very helpful, since this gives them time to mull over their thoughts. This may also lead to further correspondence that can actually become part of your development process.*

Q   I don't really have anyone to talk to about my work. Where should I turn?

A   *If you have no peers or suitable work colleagues, you may have to turn to your family. We've already warned against talking to your mum. But if you have kids, it can be very rewarding (and frustrating) to try and explain to them what you're attempting to do, as they're bound to have a completely different outlook. So be prepared for difficult and rather obscure feedback. And don't be surprised if they ask you a question that you find you can't answer. If that happens, it usually means they've put their finger on something about your work that needs fixing.*

17

Don't do lunch

Drink too much, stay up late, take the morning off, get up at 4 a.m., do all the wrong things and *then* start being creative.

In the middle of the day you should either be working obsessively or recovering from a night on the tiles.

By avoiding all the usual times for eating and sleeping, you can learn to step outside the normal social timetable. One of Bruce Mau's statements in his inspiring *Incomplete Manifesto for Growth* is: 'Stay up late. Strange things happen when you've gone too far, been up too long, worked too hard, and you're separated from the rest of the world.' Certainly it's important to be persistent when attacking a creative problem and to keep working even when you and everyone else feel like giving up. If you push yourself – don't bother having that break, going to lunch or heading for bed – eventually something will happen.

Working alone at night can have strange effects. The combination of silence, the dark and a sense that the rest of the world is asleep can definitely throw you in on yourself – and give rise to thoughts and feelings that you might not have access to during the day. Charles Dickens was a notorious night-owl, but instead of sitting in

Here's an idea for you...

Instead of being at your desk at 9 a.m., bright eyed and bushy tailed, try drinking all day instead, staying up until four in the morning and behaving quite badly (and yes, we are being serious). Obviously there are consequences in adopting this creative strategy. First, you'll have less time for work, because you've wasted it arsing about. You'll also be challenging social norms – your employers may well disapprove of liquid lunches. The good news is that the periods that you do work should have a furious intensity about them. By leaving things to the last minute and generally disrupting your usual working pattern, you'll inevitably start looking at the world in a different way. You'll also have to deal with the hangovers and feeling less than good. But strange things will spring to mind when you're in that tired, fuzzy state.

his room working on the next great novel, he'd actually get out and about in the wee small hours and walk for miles. Many of the characters who inhabited his fiction are drawn from his encounters with strange folk miles from home in the middle of the night.

Night-walking can allow you to see your local neighbourhood in a very different light. You meet a different type of person at three in the morning, and probably a few animals you wouldn't see during the day. Obviously, there's the fear that you might be mugged or find yourself in a difficult situation with a complete stranger – but that's part of the creative exercise. You can use that fear to take you to places you wouldn't otherwise go. And working your way through a strange and difficult situation is always going to give rise to creative material and memories that you can draw on later.

Speaking personally, if we, the authors (that's Rob and Tim, by the way – nice to meet you) weren't night-walkers, we would have never gone fishing for tuna in the Atlantic, never met the Asian guys in Amsterdam who thought we were undercover cops, never gone home with the French Canadian poetry-loving charity worker (and his bottle of laudanum). Rob would not have fallen in Lake Geneva and Tim would never have had his picture taken with the warthog and jar of marmalade. All of these incidents led to new ideas for projects and new ways of thinking about interaction – and also cemented our creative relationship.

You don't have to be drunk to master the gentle art of going nowhere in particular and bumping into things. Try IDEA 28, *Drift*.

Try another idea…

Staying up late, drinking too much and then sleeping in is, of course, another great way of missing lunch. It's amazing how many great artists were also piss-artists (Francis Bacon, Dylan Thomas, Kingsley Amis, Richard Burton…). In the case of French intellectual Guy Debord (co-founder of the Situationist International), drinking actually became a key part of his art: 'First like everyone, I appreciated the effect of slight drunkenness. Then very soon I grew to like what lies beyond violent drunkenness, when one has passed that stage: a magnificent and terrible peace, the true taste of the passage of time. Although in the first decades I may have allowed my self have slight indications to appear once or twice a week, it is a fact that I have been continuously drunk for periods of several months; and the rest of the time I still drank a lot.'

'Always make the effort to take things one step beyond.'
MICHAEL IAN KAYE, designer

Defining idea…

How did it go?

Q **It's all very well recommending the creative upside of hedonism, but what happens when the drugs wear off?**

A *Britart poster boy Damien Hirst has lots to say on this subject in his book* On The Way to Work. *Here's just a teaser: 'I had the best two years of my life taking drugs and drinking with Keith Allen....There'd be loads of other people there who'd be going "Have you got any more drugs" and we'd go "No". And we used to love it. They'd go "Well I'm going home". "Well fucking go home then. We're not. We're staying out. Cause we love this bit." The best bit. Our favourite bit. The drugs wearing off. You fucking hate yourself. It's fucking awful. But I'd rather be awful with my mates than be fucking awful on my own in bed...it's fantastic to feel that bad and to realise there's nothing to feel bad about. To feel all those bad things and then to know it's totally unreal.'*

Q **Nobody wants to employ an alcoholic, do they?**

A *No. But the kind of drinking we're talking about is all in the spirit of experimentation and play. If you develop a serious dependency, your work will inevitably suffer. To take the example of Damien Hirst, quoted above, his creative output declined dramatically while he battled with drink and drugs. We can all think of talented people who failed to fulfil their early promise through dissipation (Peter Cook, anyone?). So, please, be careful out there.*

18

Don't reinvent the wheel

When pre-fab can mean pretty fabulous.

Not everything you do has to be an original prototype — imagine if every car you ever owned had to be built from scratch.

If the title of this chapter sounds a bit of a cliché, that's because it is. Clichés often start life as useful shorthand for summing up ideas or situations in a succinct way that everyone can understand. So don't be too quick to write them off. Take 'not seeing the wood for the trees'. It's actually a rather snazzy and useful description for what is quite a subtle point.

Quite a lot of the time, we all think in clichés. Our brains and our imaginations operate in pretty much the same way, and our creativity works along very common lines. A lot of the ideas you have will inevitably be generic and not original. But they're none the worse for that. They can still be very useful building blocks to play with.

Here's an idea for you...

When thinking about making a simple presentation or telling a story for the first time, call upon tried and trusted techniques and formats that have stood the test of time. Use these as the spine of your work – and then add your own twists and distinctive embellishments.

It's a waste of time always forging completely new and original components for your creative projects. Often, it's how you put your thoughts together that really counts. If you don't believe us, try some flower arranging. Go and buy a couple of dozen bog-standard daffodils or roses. Now spend an hour or so thinking about different ways of arranging them. Start with a plain vase on the table and work your way up from there until you've thought of at least 52 different arrangements (there could be a book in that). Do silly arrangements. Do highly technical ones (involving balancing acts, maybe?). Use different containers or coloured water.

Incidentally, flower arranging has become a seriously creative (and lucrative) business in recent years. Recent innovations in the industry (we kid you not) include placing flowers at very precise angles, even placing them in glass vases of fizzy water – upside down!

What we hope you learn from our daft daffodil exercise is that different arrangements of common elements can produce highly original tones and textures.

Another great example of this is twelve-bar blues. The chord sequence is fantastically simple, and easy to play on the piano or guitar. But something happens to this structure when a player who knows about timing and frequency, volume and tone gets hold of it. A great blues artist uses the simple building blocks of the chord sequence to 'play' and explore many different voices and moods.

We've used that term 'building blocks' twice now, and there's a lot be said for noodling around with a few Lego bricks every now and again – even as an adult. In fact, a good team exercise is to give everyone in the office the same limited set of Lego bricks (no more than ten) and see who can come up with the most highly original construction or presentation.

Without even knowing it, we all fall into familiar routines in our creative lives. The key is understanding which bits are underpinning our creativity – and which bits are preventing us from innovating. IDEA 29, *Familiar paths, tracks and runs*, could help.

Try another idea...

Writing computer code can be a bit like playing with Lego (indeed, you can now 'program' your Lego constructions with a product called Mindstorms – itself a great creative tool). Programmers often have to make a choice about whether to reuse code from a previous project or write something afresh. Naïve programmers often like to dive in every time and make something new. This is often because one's first programming project is usually very simple and small – and so starting from scratch isn't very taxing, and you feel like you're learning along the way. But when it comes to bigger, multi-part projects, these people are sunk. They're simply overwhelmed by the workload of constantly reinventing the wheel every day for months.

We recommend therefore that you break this bad habit of originality for originality's sake very early on, when you're taking baby steps in the world of creativity. It will stand you in good stead later.

'Man invented the car but the car – out of pure malevolence no doubt – changed the history of the world by reinventing man.'
HARRY CREWS, US urban planner

Defining idea...

Q   Why shouldn't I try something mould-breaking? Surely originality has to count for something?

A   Of course. Consider the sculpture Bicycle Wheel, *by Marcel Duchamp (an inspirational figure, well worth boning up about). He 'reinvented the wheel' by quite literally turning it on its head (and sticking it onto a stool). There's nothing new or original about the two everyday items. It's how they're arranged that has turned it into art.*

Q   I just feel like I'm recycling ideas that have all been done before. How is that creative?

A   They haven't been done by you. That's the important thing. And there's always room for a better or contemporary version of something that's been done before. If you want proof, go down to your local DIY superstore and take a look at the wheelbarrows. Some are metal, some plastic. Some have wheels, others have spheres (the wheel reinvented!). Despite centuries of wheelbarrow design based on pretty much the same fixed mechanical principles, the world of wheelbarrows is still a diverse and creative space! In terms of storytelling, it's often said that there are only eight (Or is it seven? Or nine?) basic storylines that are universal. For example: man meets woman, they fall in love, society/family disapproves, but love triumphs. Or another: son falls out with father, both have a bad time apart, crisis or impending death leads to father and son reunited. (This one has been rehashed by Disney any number of times, by the way. And why? Because it works.) And look how many books there are!

19

Make your own tools

If you avoid using the same tools as everyone else, you'll be that little bit different. If you try to use soft cheese as a hammer, you'll probably be unique.

Despite using a pen or pencil every day of your life, you've probably never thought of making one — have you?!

As kids, we experiment a lot with different types of writing – chalk on the pavement, sticks in the sand, crayons on the living room wall, graffiti on park benches, peeing in the snow...

And as we get a bit older we often get a bit choosier (and fetishistic) about our writing implements – cherishing a special 'exam' pen, rearranging felt tip pens in particular colour sequences, using different coloured inks in our fountain pens, using calligraphic pens or Rotring pens, etc. If this is not exactly 'making' our own pens, it's certainly a highly developed form of customisation and personalisation. Somewhere along the line, most of us lose this passion for pens, though, and just use the first biro we can find.

Here's an idea for you...
You should never forget that your word-processing software package of choice has been 'made' for you – and the way it's been made will affect the way you process words. If you don't believe us, try using another software application to write a letter – your spreadsheet application, for example – and see how different your output turns out to be.

Our basic writing tools as adults are often foisted upon us – free of charge – via the office stationery cupboard, or picked up at conferences, found in hotels or handed out in the street by advertisers and charity workers. Perhaps it's time, therefore, you went back to having a special pen; one you have actually bought yourself and which 'suits' your style of writing. Perhaps you could go out of your way to have a pen specially made?

If this sounds too ridiculous, at least consider using something unusual or different for a day or two. Buy a pack of children's crayons and use them for all your written communications. Try making your own quill out of a bird feather. If you like a challenge, try using something that isn't even pen-like. For example, work out a mathematical alphabet that allows you to 'write' with a desktop calculator.

Defining idea...

'Tools amplify our capacities so even a small tool can make a big difference.'
BRUCE MAU, designer

Alternatively, try and consider the 'fitness for purpose' of each implement you use. What is the right pen to write with outside in the rain, or in the dark at the cinema or on top of Mount Everest? The history of the biro itself is a salutary tale in this regard. Invented by Laszlo Biro, the ballpoint pen had its first success as a writing implement for WW2 flight navigators who were fed up with their fountain pens leaking at high altitudes. Because of this rather glamorous association, after the war the ballpoint was marketed as an expensive luxury item, but failed to impress. Along came Mr Bic (actually Baron Marcel Bich), a chemical engineer, who realised he could bang out plastic biros very cheaply in very large numbers. Suddenly biro usage flourished. Interestingly, Mr Bic realised he could use his knowledge of cheap plastic moulding (i.e. tool making!) to transform the way we thought about other items too – and came up with the disposable lighter and the plastic razor.

If you don't feel confident or free enough yet to start inventing your own tools, you could always borrow some new ones from a friend. Have a look at IDEA 20, *Pick the wrong tools for the job.*

Try another idea...

Internet myth has it that both the Americans and the Russians spent a lot of time wondering what the most suitable writing implement would be to take into space. NASA spent millions developing an amazing 'space pen' that you can still buy today. The Russians just packed a few pencils.

Even if this story isn't true, it makes our point pretty well: how a creative tool gets made often defines how it is used. This is easy to forget when you're faced with something as complex as a car or a computer. Technology is often sold to us because of its supposed ability to 'set us free'. But sometimes, what we're buying is creative constraint.

'Men have become the tools of their tools.'
HENRY DAVID THOREAU

Defining idea...

Q   Aren't I in danger of having lovely new tools and nothing to show for it?

A   *We're not asking you to ignore the output you're aiming at: a painting of a dog, an article on aubergines, a birthday present. We just want you to think more about developing your own toolsets for delivering outputs. Manufacturers often 'tool up' in order to make new widgets. Indeed, it can sometimes be one of the biggest costs for a new product manufacturer. But that doesn't mean the company doesn't concentrate hard on the end product. Of course they do. Next time you have a goal in mind, challenge yourself about how you're going to deliver it. Could you make your own special brush for painting that delivers a unique effect? Could your article on aubergines be written on an aubergine? Could the birthday present you buy (or make!) be an 'experience' rather than a standard item from a shop?*

Q   If I start mucking about with new tools at work, my productivity will drop dramatically, won't it?

A   *Ye-es. So don't start with anything too critical. Leave the important ones till later. It's amazing how even the most humdrum experiences can be changed if you are forced to make or remake all the tools you use. How would your morning shower or bath change if you had to make your own soap or flannel (or, rather, 'wiping/soaping device')? It's actually very common for design students in their first year at college to be set the challenge of reinventing common tools – designing a set of cutlery, for example. Try doing that now and see how it compares with your regular set.*

20

Pick the wrong tools for the job

When is a screwdriver not a screwdriver? (You might have to think about this one...)

We've all done it. You have an urgent need for a hammer and can't find one. So you pick up a piece of wood, a heavy book or an old shoe and bash away with that.

Sometimes it does the job. Often it doesn't, and you may well go through several household items – damaging or destroying some of them – before you give in and dedicate your time to finding the hammer instead.

Either way, you've learned something about 'hammerness' – what it takes to be a good or a bad hammer – and maybe also you've developed some thoughts about why hammers aren't considered to be 'a good read' (like the heavy book) and don't necessarily make great footwear (like the shoe).

Here's an idea for you...

Choosing the 'wrong' tool might just mean choosing a new tool, or adapting something from a different discipline that might turn out to be the 'right' tool. Low-temperature physicist Nicholas Kurti used early microwave technology to create an 'Inverted Baked Alaska' (frozen meringue filled with piping hot apricot purée), described as 'sticking a spoon into Iceland and getting an eyeful of magma'. Find your own new uses for existing tools.

Hammering without a hammer is about becoming absorbed with the process rather than being obsessed with the outcome all the time. If all you care about is driving that nail in quickly, the hammer's your tool of choice. If you're seriously interested in developing your creativity, you should be inspecting closely how the nail gets driven in and why. By not using a hammer, these other aspects of your chosen activity will be made more explicit. You may even be drawn into thoughts about the 'wrong' tool you've chosen to use. If you start bashing away with a shoe, it's likely to provoke thoughts not only about its 'non-hammerness', but also about its essential 'shoeness' – why it has a heel or a tongue, how the sole flexes, whether it's made of plastic or leather, etc.

Really creative people can use this kind of activity as the jumping-off point for making all kinds of creative connections between hammers and shoes. Consider the marching hammers that Gerald Scarfe created for the movie *The Wall* – tools made for walking (like shoes!). This is Scarfe making a series of creative connections instinctively – from thematic concept to hammer, from hammer to hammer-as-marching boot:

'Roger [Waters of Pink Floyd] was saying in his piece (*The Wall*), I think, that if you wall yourself from others too much you become insensitive and a kind of machine or an automaton…so I tried to think of the most unrelenting kind of cruel symbol of that thing in mind. And so the first thing that came into

By taking out the best bits of a project, the rest can sometimes be knocked into better shape and balance. IDEA 15, *Bin your best work*, will show you how.

Try another idea…

my mind was the hammer, because it's metal, it smashes things, it's unrelenting…And then the other thing was to make it march because it has echoes of fascism and Nazism and so on. So that's how that really came about, these faceless, mindless tools of destruction just marching ever onward unrelentingly.'

It's good not to take an object for granted. Try considering it not just as a single-purpose device, but as something that you can use in many different ways – and also seeing it as a symbol. Put a sickle next to your hammer and suddenly you're invoking associations with something else entirely. (Lost? Think flag, dummy!)

It's actually a test of your ingenuity to pick up the wrong tool and still manage to do something creative with it. For example, one of the finest traditions in slapstick comedy survives thanks to the insistence of funnymen throughout the ages not to use frying pans only for frying. 'Ha! Ha! Bonk!'

Curiously, it was the absence of frying pans that forced British soldiers in North Africa to think laterally about frying their eggs without a pan. They used their jeeps and tanks instead: the combined heat of the sun and the vehicle engines turned the bonnets into perfectly adequate frying devices.

'A bell is a cup until it is struck.'
WIRE

Defining idea…

How did it go?

Q What if I can't afford new tools – even 'wrong' ones?

A   *Necessity, they say, is the mother of invention. But what we're talking about here isn't just about making do with what you've got. It's about actively ignoring the tools you're supposed to use and doing something else instead. No doubt the painter Jackson Pollock had a pretty comprehensive brush collection, but instead, one day he decided he would just drip and dribble his paint straight from the tin (presumably opening it with his screwdriver first) and thus the course of art history was changed. It didn't cost him anything (financially) to do this. Another artist, Yves Klein, sometimes used a flame-thrower instead of a brush – and also managed to persuade a number of naked women to cover themselves in paint and roll around on his canvases. You may need to work on your powers of persuasion and refer to your employment contract before attempting something like this in the office. But it proves that 'wrongness' is a pretty broad term in this context.*

Q Surely using the wrong tool for the job makes the job take longer, means I have to work harder and suggests the end result is going to suffer?

A   *Yes, if the end result you're looking for is the one you usually get, and the same one everyone else expects. If you choose a different tool to tackle the same job, even the wrong tool, the end result may be unexpectedly good (or just very broken). As the well-known motivational theorist, Abraham Maslow, once commented: 'If the only tool you have is a hammer, you will see every problem as a nail.'*

21

Swap tools with someone else

Be a complete amateur with someone else's kit.

Go ahead. Just sit down and do whatever you want to do in an unschooled, amateurish way.

Yes, first time out you'll probably produce something that's pretty rubbish. So what? You don't worry about that the first time you play a new game. Think of the first time you joined in a game of football or a school of cards or a session of Monopoly. You knew very well that it would probably take a number of rounds or matches before you really got the hang of it (assuming you were picked again). It might occur to you to get some lessons, or to read the rulebook or refer to an expert manual – but only after you've already played a few games.

But somehow, when it comes to more 'serious' creative work, we're too inhibited or embarrassed to adopt this approach. We feel we somehow need to be 'qualified' before we get even started. Frankly, the way we learn most of the life skills that parents and teachers can't really teach us is through the embarrassing and

Here's an idea for you...

Borrow a complicated piece of kit from a neighbour or friend – a hedge cutter, say, or a concrete mixer – and try and work out under your own steam how to become, if not expert, then at least adequate at trimming hedges or mixing concrete. This isn't just a boy thing, by the way – it's just as important for creative women to challenge themselves and the people around them by working with kit like this.

sometimes undermining process of trial and error. It is chiefly, therefore, fear of making mistakes, fear of embarrassing ourselves in public, of being humiliated or 'looking stupid' that stops many of us from seeing ourselves as 'creative'.

Dressing yourself up in the clothes of another is a great way of hiding – or at least muffling – that fear. By admitting straight up that you have no idea what to do with that drill or where to put that widget, you're wearing your ignorance very publicly on your sleeve and are thus free to explore.

For many people, the most obvious way to get into this exploratory frame of mind is to indulge in a little bit of untutored DIY. Challenge yourself to put up those shelves, plaster that wall, wire in those lamps. Make sure it's something you haven't really tried to do before, and start small. Probably best too to stick to tasks that aren't going to impact badly on the people you live with should things go wrong (so don't try a plumbing venture that could leave your household without hot water for a week...). On the other hand, don't let anyone tease or criticise you into giving up on the job. So what if the shelf ends up being not quite level or the door doesn't quite close properly? *That's not the point!*

What you're doing in these seemingly mundane and domestic tasks is learning the essential art of 'getting by' – solving problems as they occur and thus pushing out your learning in front of you, rather than displaying it in your wake.

Working in this way allows you to concentrate on the now and the new – and not get bogged down in the past and the known. Sometime we refer to this as working in the dark, as if that's a negative thing (although best not to try this with the power saw). But think about yourself wandering round in the pitch black with a torch for a moment. Where do you point it? Ahead of you, where you're hoping to find new things, or behind you in order to illuminate the landscape that you've already logged?

Sometimes using someone else's tools can make you less inhibited and enable you to make big bold statements in your new medium. See what's available in IDEA 46, *Tools of the trade – technology.*

Try another idea...

'All the really good ideas I ever had came to me while I was milking a cow.'
GRANT WOOD, painter

Defining idea...

How did it go?

Q **There are some moments where you just have to be an expert, aren't there? Like flying a plane...**

A *As it happens, pilots know all about working by 'the seat of their pants', i.e. using their natural instincts rather than their expertise. They develop a feel for a plane by sensing the forces exerted on it and transmitted through the pilot's seat cushion (buttock training, anyone?). If the aeroplane is perfectly balanced, neither going up nor down, nor turning, accelerating or slowing, your body won't feel a thing. When the forces go out of balance, inertia wants to move your body – and your body (mainly your arse) feels it. At this point you are literally flying by the seat of your pants with no reference to all the fancy dials and knobs that you're meant to use. Don't be afraid therefore to swap tools with anyone – and we mean anyone!*

Q **What kind of person should I swap tools with?**

A *You don't have to go very far away from your own territory in order to try something new. If you're a writer by nature, seek out a more visual and less text-centric artist and try your hand at painting pictures instead. If you're of a technical bent and build websites, have a go at tapestry – a different form of 'webbing'! Alternatively, if you're a rather sedentary person, why not experience the adrenalin rush of doing something more active? The key here is to get yourself out of any rut you may have fallen into creatively.*

22

All time is playtime

If it's daytime it must be playtime. Work out how every interaction of the day can be 'played'.

People who turn everything into a game are often portrayed as wily operators, or supercilious types who don't really take anything seriously.

But nearly every interaction you have in the world is something of a game – in most cases, you just haven't worked the rules out yet.

Gameplayers have a lot to teach us about exposing the basic working parts of any experience and identifying its creative value. If you can learn to master the 'rules' of any given situation, often it means that you can 'play' that situation more creatively each time it occurs. Not only are you staying alert to the creative potential of the moment, you're honing your critical and emotional responses. Like every good sports player, you're engaged in a programme of intensive training. And by making things hyper-real in this way, you're becoming hyper-sensitive to your surroundings.

What we're describing here is not unlike what happens to you the first time you put on a portable music player and go walking around a big city. Suddenly your life

Here's an idea for you...

Constantly analyse your action, to become more self-aware. Thinking of even the most inane tasks as training can allow you to perceive value in them. When you poured yourself a coffee or tea this morning, did you do it 'better' than yesterday? Was your pouring action smooth? Did you pour from a greater height? Was there any spillage? It sounds silly, but an Olympic pole vaulter will be asking these kinds of questions every time he or she trains (not about coffee-pouring, obviously).

has a soundtrack and you feel like you're acting in a movie. Perhaps you start to walk like John Travolta. Every passer-by is potentially another actor in your movie. Every moment is pregnant with the possibility of being a 'big scene'. Try it and see how it changes your perception of what you thought was a familiar landscape. Try walking the same route to two radically different soundtracks and see what kind of emotions and thoughts each one elicits.

In the last couple of years, digital artists such as Blast Theory have taken this idea one step further by developing ways of playing an online role-playing game even as you carry on your normal life around town – as portayed in their project *Uncle Roy All Around You* (for details of how to play, go to www.uncleroyallaroundyou.co.uk). When you take part in games like these you definitely look at everything with fresh eyes and lose your complacency about everday existence. Suddenly everything that happens has to fit in with your sense of the game, and thus every experience takes on a new sense.

In a way, many people are already doing something similar in their lives by not only adding a soundtrack to the day with iPods and Walkmans, but using mobile text messaging to communicate with 'players', setting themselves 'missions' throughout the day, acquiring 'kit' and winning 'powers' or 'rewards'. All the basic ingredients of a PlayStation game like *Tomb Raider* or *Splinter Cell* are there. (Getting to know your way around a PlayStation is *de rigueur* for creative people these days, by the way.)

Try now to map out a typical day of yours as if it were a console game. You may well reveal patterns that you hadn't seen before. Perhaps a new soundtrack will emerge. You may also find that you achieve more distance from events in which you're usually immersed. By seeing it all as a game, you can stay above it all and therefore learn to be more dispassionate about assessing the value of various experiences.

Getting better at games, of course, requires practice and repetition. You may think that you've already got enough routine and repetition in your life, and you may feel hemmed in or bored by it. But ultimately you'll gain an instinctive understanding of such high falutin' concepts as 'flow' and 'immersion' – those moments in both games and real life when you feel completely at ease in terms of your concentration, your awareness, your appreciation, your instincts, physical ability and skill level; in fact, exactly the kind of feeling you want others to have when they're immersed in something you've created.

Since you're being more playful in your life, we're expecting to hear a lot more laughter from you – and the people around you. For the importance of being frivolous, go to IDEA 24, *Laugh a lot*.

Try another idea...

'Life must be lived as play.'
PLATO

Defining idea...

95

Q **Most games, particularly computer games, seem to be based around solving puzzles of one kind or another. I spend my life problem solving and I hate puzzles, so why should I be interested in games?**

A *We're not asking you to fill up your leisure time playing games (well, maybe just a bit). What we're suggesting is more fundamental, with the emphasis on 'fun'. Trying to reorganise your creative process so that it becomes more game-like, by inventing arbitrary rules, for example, is what you should aim for. If you enjoy what you do, chances are other people will enjoy it too.*

Q **Playing games just makes me better at games. My creative life hasn't changed at all. Why not?**

A *Well, we'd claim you're just not paying attention to what's going on when you're playing games. Here are some pointers that poker player and writer Larry W. Phillips feels can be taken from the card table and applied to life:*

1. *take the long view*
2. *once you commit to a hand, play it strong*
3. *don't throw in good money after bad*
4. *if you think you're beat, get out.*

23

Play your part

**Using role-play in your daily life can help you discover
things about yourself and other people.**

Most of us at some time of our life have
wondered what it might be like to be
someone else.

It may be a character from history who you identify with or a best friend you
admire; whoever it is, it's entirely natural to try and emulate that person. By acting
like other people, we are trying to discover a little more about ourselves. It starts at
an early age, imitating mum and dad: the obvious way to learn what it might be
like to be an adult (or not, as the case may be). Even when we think we've done all
our growing up, we still use role-play in order to develop our skills and build up our
experience. For example, most business managers don't receive much formal
training about how to manage. Instead, they learn from their own bosses. They 'act
out the part' of being a business manager until they've gained enough experience
to actually become the part.

Here's an idea for you...

Take a trip to the zoo and see what you can learn about body language, facial expressions, mannerisms, social behaviour, eating, goal-based activity, basic desire and playfulness that you can adopt for a while in your own life. Be a stick insect for a day – very still, blending into the background with simple, slow needs. Be a gorilla the next day – park yourself in the centre of every situation, stare, eat noisily and scratch yourself a lot. (Ah, you've done that already!)

Human beings love to copy each other. When we talk to someone with a strong regional accent, we sometimes find ourselves talking the same way. Sometimes we'll even subconsciously adopt their mannerisms and verbal tics. Yet despite these natural acts of mimicry, pretending to be someone else is pretty much frowned upon in conventional society. Not being authentically yourself is seen as insincere or devious. Adopting a false identity is the practice of criminals and crazy people – or even worse, actors!

Thus, when we tell you it's good to indulge in a bit of role-play, we're assuming it's something you'll have to do surreptitiously; that is, unless a whole group of you decide to experiment in this way together (like a comedy double act or theatre company might do).

The kind of play-acting we're suggesting isn't wigs and make-up. It's more internalised – a form of creative projection whereby you consider how situations might play out differently if you were actually somebody else. For example, in a particularly stressful meeting, where someone accuses you of some cock-up, you might typically become defensive and touchy (like Tim). But if today you've decided to be a more silent and laid-back person (like Rob), you'll almost certainly end up in a different place by the end of the meeting – both in terms of how you reacted to events and how you moved past them. This exercise, then, is very much about not being your normal self – and thus hopefully becoming clearer about who your normal self is.

Perhaps you have more than one 'normal self', depending on who you're with and what you're doing. If so, try to pick just one to play. Say to yourself: 'Today I'll be the petulant child my mum knows so well.' Or: 'Today I'll be an *ingénue*. Tomorrow I'll be a critic.'

Another way of shaking things up is to experiment with your own prejudices about gender-based behaviour. If you're a man, spend some time thinking what you'd be like as a woman, and how you'd behave. If you're a woman, try and think like a man (trust us, men do think occasionally…).

Many people swap genders on the internet and happily chat away with strangers as Glenda when doing the washing-up as Glenn. In most cases, no harm is done and something can be learnt (not all people who take on fake online personas are paedophiles and sex offenders).

Role-play can also be about simply changing your perspective. Check out IDEA 11, *Look at things another way*, for ways to do this.

Try another idea…

'Play is the exultation of the possible.'
MARTIN BUBER, philosopher

Defining idea…

99

In our case, we actually created a completely bogus female character on the Web called Caroline Close, who had her own webcam and would mail you every day if you wanted her to. This was envisaged as a form of interactive drama, but for many people who played it, it also became a form of creative role-play where they could rehearse making friends with a complete stranger online without having to live with the consequences in their real lives. You can still try it at www.onlinecaroline.com.

Putting yourself into other people's shoes can really help when it comes to developing new work. For example, if you were designing a chicken hutch, it would be obvious to make it appeal to the chicken owner who is paying for it. But a really good hutch designer will also spend some time thinking like the other people who may have some influence on the purchase – the partner, the children, the neighbour. And the best hutch designer of all will also think like a chicken – and a fox!

Always try to remain alert to all the possible players in any given situation.

Q **This kind of role-playing just makes me look like either I'm showing off or I'm mad. Am I doing it right?**

How did it go?

A *You don't have to completely change who you are. Be more surreptitious than that. Think of it like a musician choosing to play in a certain style for a while. Would you, for example, want to play bass guitar like Paul McCartney or like Bootsie Collins? (If you don't know who Bootsie Collins is, find out!) Either choice doesn't change the fact that it's you who is playing. You're just experimenting with someone else's style, that's all.*

Q **I'm rubbish at acting and I like being me. Can I stop now, please?**

A *OK, why don't you tone it down a bit? Perhaps you could just play around a little bit with the vocabulary you use. Pay attention to words that you overuse and then ruthlessly eradicate them. Get a crush on other words (like 'melange', 'yeoman' or 'weird'). This isn't too demanding or silly – and it may well turn you into a more concise and entertaining communicator.*

24

Laugh a lot

Strategies for having a giggle without becoming the class clown. Other than skulking in the back row, that is.

If you can't look like you're enjoying your creative work, it's highly unlikely that anyone else is going to take much pleasure in it either.

It's a myth that all great art requires the artist to suffer. Yes, creative people tend to be sensitive to the world around them, often tackling serious issues such as poverty, love and death. But that doesn't mean the artist is necessarily a joyless, glum person. Far from it. Just witness the chatty, wild social groupings that often occur when artists congregate.

Whenever you're gathering people together around a creative project, you should always try to inject a bit of this party atmosphere. We humans love to laugh. Whenever people are asked to describe the perfect partner or list their reasons for falling in love, the most common personal attribute cited is 'he/she makes me laugh'. Adults laugh on average seventeen times a day (apparently); kids laugh at least twice as much again. Quite why we laugh less as we grow up hasn't yet been explained.

Here's an idea for you...

Start a laughter club. Originated by Madan Kataria, an Indian physician, laughter clubs are now popular all over India, where people meet outdoors early in the morning for 15 or 20 minutes to practise 'laughter yoga'. The trademark 'ho-ho-ha-ha-ha' laugh is punctuated by hand claps to get the blood circulating, repeated at regular intervals. You could also try the 'cocktail laugh' (the kind of snickering you emit over drinks) or the 'lion laugh' (tongue stuck out, hands posed like lion paws, and a roar).

It seems so natural, but laughing is a complex response to the world around us, and it's a facility that most other animal species don't have. So cherish it. It's also a social phenomenon. While it's possible to laugh by yourself when reading a funny book or watching a funny film, research from laughter experts such as Professor Robert R. Provine suggests that people are about thirty times more likely to laugh when they're in a social situation than when alone.

Laughter is also contagious – dangerously so, at times. In Tanganyika in 1962, a group of schoolgirls laughed so much and for so long that it eventually infected not only the whole of the local community, but also several adjoining towns. The epidemic was so severe that it required the closing of schools, and it lasted for six months! (It was no laughing matter.)

Although we're not suggesting that you and your work should provoke that kind of reaction, encouraging laughter is a good tactic. Most successful presentations and 'pitches', be it communicating ideas or selling stuff, are those where everyone in the room is having a good time, and include both serious, thought-provoking moments and humorous episodes that produce shared laughter.

Humour often comes from placing things that don't normally go together: the serious and the silly, the logical and the absurd (what serious people know as 'incongruity'). Similarly, many jokes are based on the principle that the audience is expecting one outcome but gets another – it's the surprise that makes us laugh.

If you really are feeling down and are incapable of laughter, don't force it. Instead, read IDEA 49, *Come back in the morning.*

Try another idea...

There are many reasons why we laugh – not all of them positive. Consider the difference between laughing *with* and laughing *at* someone. You should generally avoid the latter – although telling a funny story against someone (preferably someone not in the room) who is stupid or has experienced some kind of bad luck is a great unifier. It's the feeling of superiority that comes from thinking someone else is the butt of a joke that wins the attention and loyalty from your audience. Be careful, though, to pick your targets carefully.

Humour is also a great way to generate relief in a difficult situation. Film-makers, for example, often build up the tension or suspense only to break it with a side comment or comic incident (think of James Bond's silly quips after each and every fight scene). This device allows the viewer to relieve pent-up emotions and get ready for the next build-up.

'As soon as you have made a thought, laugh at it.'
LAO TZU

Defining idea...

All stories or situations create tension to a greater or lesser degree. Laughter is nature's way of cleansing our system – it's an extremely healthy built-in stress buster. It can also be a powerful tool for spreading disorder (as in Tanganyika) and undermining authority (as in satire). If you feel your creative life is being stifled by working in an environment that's too well ordered and secure, acting the clown can break things up very effectively.

Many people actually find circus clowns very threatening. Part of that is the sense of anarchy that clowns possess. They are the only circus performers, for example, who are allowed to perform their act outside of the main ring, in among the audience.

Do you have a 'main ring' in which everyone you know performs? What would happen if you stepped out of it?

Q   **How can I be taken seriously if I'm always laughing and clowning around?**

How did it go?

A   *'Playing the fool' is a centuries old tradition and is a very serious business indeed. Kings and queens employed court jesters precisely because they wanted to spread a litte unease and to combat complacency among the courtiers. Jesters and fools could also be counted on to come up with a different kind of advice and 'wisdom' than one gets from the sycophancts and yes-men who often surround powerful people. Could you see yourself in this role? Could your laughter be less about silliness for silliness' sake, and more about making a point?*

Q   **I'm just not funny. I've got about as much levity as an unmade bread (bread – bed, geddit? See what I mean?). What should I do?**

A   *Why not team up with someone who is? Maybe you're better off playing the 'straight man' (or woman). Morecambe & Wise, arguably the UK's most successful comedy duo, started out copying the comic routines of Abbott & Costello, with Eric Morecambe as the straight man. Only when they reversed their roles did they start to achieve success.*

25

Be childlike

Spot the difference between adult fun and child fun (and they say that size doesn't matter...).

You used to be one, you know — I kid you not. And you should never forget it.

In fact, you should do your best to remember not just that you were once a child, but also how it felt and how you behaved. If this is difficult, find yourself a small child and watch them closely (with the parents' permission, naturally). In particular, watch them at play and try to relate this to the game techniques and forms of play that you used to enjoy as a child.

Part of what's interesting about this process should be the growing realisation that a lot of your adult creative work is actually replaying a lot of the things you liked doing as a kid in some form or other. Not only are you still drawing from the same sources of inspiration (subconsciously, maybe), but you're probably still drawn to the same creative spaces, the same situations and sometimes even the same sort of people who you liked hanging out with then.

Here's an idea for you...

Go back and take a look at the places where you used to play. Don't drown yourself in nostalgia, mind. What you should be noting is both what has remained the same and what's changed now that you're a grown-up. Think back for a moment – did you have a favourite spot where you liked playing? Was it outside in the garden? Was it your bedroom at home? Perhaps even at school? While writing this idea we both confessed that as kids we liked playing outside in flower beds and shrubberies, setting up war scenes with toy soldiers. Perhaps this shared (but also rather remote and megalomaniacal) childhood experience is the real reason why we like working together.

There are certainly also some aspects of childlike behaviour you may have forsaken as an adult – both the good bits and the bad bits. For example, you may have lost some powers of concentration that it would be good to get back – the ability to get obsessed about something and spend the whole day fiddling with one particular toy, a cup of milk, a song, a story...

You may also have learnt how to modulate your personality so that you don't have so many tantrums and don't 'throw your rattle out of the pram'. This is generally a good thing. But then again – perhaps you aren't having enough tantrums as an adult to ensure that you get the space you need to be creative (that's mental space, not pram space).

Certainly you should have broadened your vocabulary, which should be useful to you as a creative person. Don't confuse this, however, with being a more effective communicator. If you listen to kids talking – on public transport, in other people's houses, in your own house – you'll quickly realise that their limited vocabulary doesn't stop them tackling very complex concepts. In fact, their use of simple words, slang, gesture, repetitions and the music of their voices should be a challenge to your adult ideas of what effective communication is.

In the same way, many abstract painters sometimes use childlike simplicity to convey very complex emotions and thoughts. And what is a common reaction to that kind of art?

'Blimey, my four year-old could've done that.'

Trying to explain your creative ideas in simple language to a small child is a great way of getting a new perspective on your work. For other ways, look at IDEA 11, *Look at things another way.*

Try another idea...

'Look at life with the eyes of a child.'
HENRI MATISSE

Defining idea...

111

How did it go?

Q **I want to create work for adults, not kiddy stuff. Why should I regress?**

A *J.K. Rowling probably started out writing exclusively for children, but that hasn't stopped millions of adults reading Harry Potter. Very often there's no distinction between creative work for adults and that for kids (apart from the sex and violence).*

Q **Can I apply a childlike approach to my grown-up workplace?**

A *Some creative management gurus push the idea of grown-ups returning to the sandpit as a place to come up with challenging new ideas. Beware of this. Sure, kids like to play in sandpits (and on the beach in summer) but it's never just about the enjoyment of the sand. Your pleasure is always relative to who else is in the pit, the position of the pit relative to the things that make you feel secure (such as your home and your family), and the type of toys and tools that surround you. Corporate sandpits are never going recreate these subtle nuances. And anyway, while play itself can be shared, the enjoyment of play is personal and specific.*

Q **I acted like a child, and so everybody treated me like one. Why didn't it feel right?**

A *Despite our obvious enthusiasm for the energy and innocence of youth, we do recognise that being a kid isn't all good. For example, most kids simply don't have power or authority to make things happen, and that's something you should definitely value and nurture. You also have experience and skills that a child could never have – and more patience and stamina. If you hold on to these adult qualities, you're not likely to get pushed around by others.*

26

Boys' toys and girls' gadgets

Is that a miniaturised digital flip-chart in your pocket or are you just pleased to see me? Take grown-up gadgets and start treating them like all your other accessories.

Time to tip your toys out. Take a good look at the things you carry around with you every day in your suitcase, in your handbag, in your pockets.

We all carry a lot of baggage around with us to help us get through a normal day. Much of it is seemingly essential equipment (wallet, keys, cards), others bits are less so (make-up, books, games). It's time you took an audit of all these little portable accessories and started to assess more carefully how often you use them and what you use them for. In particular, we want to know where your mobile phone or electronic diary fits into this picture. Is it an essential or a luxury for you? Do you use it often or only when absolutely necessary? For business or for pleasure?

Here's an idea for you...

If you haven't got into mobile gadgetry yet, give it a try. And this isn't just an excuse to make or receive more voice calls. These babies can be used for so much more these days: texting, taking photos, playing games, playing music, Web surfing, emailing, downloading and so on. So go buy one as soon as you can. Extravagant? Think of it as you would about buying a new pair of shoes or an expensive lipstick. Like shoes, you are allowed to have more than one phone. And in the future, you'll wear these things rather than carry them. Phones will become earrings. Your watch will double up as a camera. MP3 players will be stitched into jackets. Already there are geeks out there who wear USB memory sticks as necklaces – it's true!

We ask you this because your emotional response to these newfangled pocket-sized gadgets and your usage of them can say a lot about the kind of creative person you are.

So drag out everything you've got that's small and pocketable and lay it out on a table. Now write down how may times you use each thing a day, give each one a mark out of ten in terms of practical importance and also mark them based on your sentimental attachment to them (photos of loved ones, for example). Generally, build up a detailed picture of your personal relationship with your belongings. Importantly, also identify the things that you use in a number of different ways for various tasks, and those which are pretty much single-use devices. For example, you probably think of door keys as useful only for opening doors – but people often use them for opening other things, such as beer bottles and cardboard boxes (and for sawing through string and cord – a tip from Tim).

What we're trying to get you to do here is gain a deeper understanding of how you like to accessorise your creative processes. We all do it. We decorate our days with random communication processes and interactions that often involve putting our hands in our pockets or digging something out of our handbags. And with the mobile technology revolution that is currently taking place, we're at a moment in time when that accessorising and decorating process is going to be much richer and multifarious.

If you keep abreast of how quickly the world of technology is changing, you'll end up with a whole lot more toys and concepts to play with. Get a flavour from IDEA 46, *Tools of the trade – technology.*

Try another idea...

'A new gadget that lasts only five minutes is worth more than an immortal work that bores everyone.'
FRANCIS PICABIA, French painter/illustrator/designer

Defining idea...

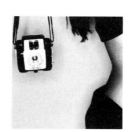

How did
it go?

Q   Gadgets are just for boys really, aren't they?

A   *Absolutely not. Mobile devices are a natural accessory for women too. Given
their shape and their ability to vibrate instead of simply 'ring', they also
have a certain appeal for women that is closed to most men (think about
it). And in the future women are much more likely to 'wear' mobile devices
than men (you can stop thinking about it now). Mobile technology is also
changing relationships between men and women, with texting and wireless
network technologies such as Bluetooth being used for virtual sex
encounters, blind-dating and one-off encounters with strangers on trains
(this is called 'toothing'). Women are also using mobile cameras and
'moblogging' to keep a record of who they are with at all times (the
number plate of the taxi they're getting into, etc.) as a personal security
system. Teenage women are avid texters and chatters. Need we say more?*

**Q   The problem with mobiles is that they keep interrupting my flow with
unwanted calls and messages. Is that counterproductive or what?**

A   *It's true that many people of a certain age still keep their mobile phone
switched off unless they are making a call. But if you want to be 'always on',
then you have to be 'always interruptible'. Younger people seem to be better
at this. Instead of making a plan on Monday to meet up on Wednesday
evening, they'll organise their social life on the fly with streams of texting
and phonecalling, polling everybody's current location and activity, and
spotting opportunities for ad-hoc meetings. Try it. In the near future you'll
be able to leave voice and text messages in specific locations like a crumb
trail of where you've been, for others to pick up later. Creative people will
find wonderful things to do with these new technologies.*

27

Thinking inside the box

You've got more ideas and sparks of inspiration than you have time to deal with them. Find out where to store those ideas you haven't got round to yet.

The most obvious way to sort your ideas into categories and box them up is to institute a filing system. Problem is, filing — as we all know — is one of the most boring activities known to man.

A huge proportion of the stuff we put into filing cabinets never sees the light of day again. The main reason for this is we don't bother making notes about 'why' we're filing anything. And there's never an action point assigned to the things we squirrel away. We actively decide in most cases to do absolutely nothing about the things we thought were worth saving from the bin. If you're not careful, all you'll have to show for keeping a whole load of newspaper cuttings is a pile of newspaper cuttings and no new ideas.

Here's an idea for you...

If digital displays are not your thing, revert back to old-fashioned cabinets. Collectors of the past were very fond of display cabinets for showing off vast hordes of stones, shells, bugs and butterflies. Many of us still like to decorate our homes with this kind of stuff. Create your own display cabinet, containing whatever you consider to be interesting, beautiful or talismanic. Or start a collection of one particular type of thing. Tim started keeping the sticky labels from fruit for a while, until he came across someone who was doing the same thing online in a much more thorough way.

The way out of this is to make the filing cabinet your playground. Crucially, your thinking about all the things you store up in little boxes needs to be associative; you need to develop tools and techniques for mixing and matching your clippings, organising them into thematic clusters or charting them on a map in some way.

Technology can help with this. There are some great tools out there – usually offering some kind of database structure that allows you to scan in items and then tag them with ratings, keywords or labels of some kind. At the click of a button you can then change your 'view' into the database, so that the things that might appeal to your current train of creative thought right now are closer to hand while the less interesting stuff is further away. Digital music tools like iTunes work exactly like this in that you can even get the computer to randomly generate playlists from your collection based on music type, your personal ratings, number of times a tune has been played recently, length of tune, etc. (Hmm. Not that random, then, but you can see what we're driving at.)

To make this kind of ongoing filing and retrieval system work really well, you have to get into the discipline of annotating and 'tagging' everything you come into contact with as you go along. A simple way to understand how this might work is to sign up to the Amazon online store (www.amazon.com) and start adding items to your Wishlist section. You don't have to buy anything. You just log your interest and, as you do it, your Wishlist grows. You can annotate this with reasons 'why' you want this item.

What could you do with all that media you generate on holiday – the photos, the postcards, the souvenirs? Get some pointers in IDEA 33, *Creative tourism.*

Try another idea...

Very quickly you will have created a list of things that interest you, all sat alongside each other. Connections and themes might grow as you sift back through this. And since your Wishlist is 'free to air', all your friends can quickly discover what to buy you for your birthday. The online phenomenon that is blogging is pretty much about this same process too.

At this point, you might be wondering what this has to do with boxes. But really, all we're talking about is collecting stuff and playing with it inside digital display panels rather than inside wooden or metal boxes.

'Shadow boxes become poetic theatres or settings wherein are metamorphosed the element of a childhood pastime.'
JOSEPH CORNELL

Defining idea...

How did it go?

Q   **Putting things in a box seems like putting a boundary on my creativity rather than letting things float free. Isn't it restrictive?**

A   *Yes and no. It's true that boxing things up is one way of getting rid of them or killing them off (think of your bin, or a coffin). But you may just be laying them down to mature like fine wine. Or consider it as a way of signing off a chapter, marking a line in the sand as if to say 'this far and no farther with this idea'. Many great artists have done fantastically creative things with boxes. Joseph Cornell and Joseph Beuys are both seminal artists in this regard. They use 'enclosure' to encapsulate a particular time and/or issue, or to frame something in a particular way (as propaganda, maybe). And they also freeze their thinking about a particular issue in more than one dimension. Could you do that?*

Q   **You can't keep a record of everything you do in your life, can you?**

A   *Probably not. But you can certainly have a good try. Consider the Microsoft-backed project called My Life Bits, which involves a man called Gordon Bell capturing a lifetime's worth of articles, books, cards, CDs, letters, memos, papers, photos, pictures, presentations, home movies, videotaped lectures and voice recordings, and storing them digitally. He is now paperless, and is beginning to capture phone calls, IM transcripts, television and radio too. It takes a hell of a lot of smart technology to allow this to happen. But in a few years it'll be possible to store sound recording of every minute of our lives on hard disk and make it searchable. It will probably take magic to make this interesting though.*

28

Drift

Learning the gentle art of going nowhere in particular and bumping into things can help spark your creativity – wherever it is you find yourself.

Now this is the easiest creative exercise you're ever going to get: just stumble around in any direction and make it look like you really don't know what you're doing.

Of course, on any given morning that's pretty much what we're all doing already!

There's a fine tradition of this stumbling and bumbling within all forms of art, but this key idea of 'drift' or *dérive* has probably been best employed and explained by Guy Debord, French intellectual and founding father of the art movement Situationist International. *Dérive* for Debord usually involved bouncing around Paris drunk, following some deliberately vague rules.

Here's an idea for you... **Go for a walk online. Use an arbitrary system of clicks and links to lose yourself entirely in the Web, and confront yourself with loads of thought-provoking online material along the way.**

These included:

- Drop your usual motives for movement and action, relations, work and leisure activities.

- The average duration of a *dérive* is a day, considered as the time between two periods of sleep.

- The spatial field of the *dérive* may be precisely delimited or vague.

Although this sounds suspiciously like not doing much at all, it was highly political in its day, coming to the fore during the Paris riots of 1968.

By deliberately not having any specific creative aim or output in mind from the outset, Debord and others were attempting to remove themselves from the 'madeness' of modern life, the capitalistic urge to always turn creativity into product and experience life only as consumption (or shopping). By avoiding the manufactured elements of your experience (your schooling, your class, your job) you can perceive something more authentic and 'real'. This idea has roots in surrealism, and several other French '-isms' besides. As such, we're not recommending you take it too seriously. (For Debord, it led to links with international terrorist groups, alcoholism and suicide.)

Defining idea... **'The idea is to have no idea. Get lost. Get lost in the landscape.'**
MALCOLM MORLEY, painter and sculptor

But there are two basic concepts that you might like to experiment with. The first is the idea of spurning the straight and narrow for the playful and lateral. Learn to love the free associative wander. The second is to play with the idea of useless maps and dabble in a bit of psychogeography: 'the study of specific effects of the geographical environment, consciously organised or not, on the emotions and behaviour of individuals'. Debord's example of a psychogeographic excursion was to use a map of London as his means for navigating a region of Germany. By doing so, he didn't really know where he was going, so his route would be random and his response to the geography of the German town would be spontaneous.

Check out game playing in **IDEA 22, *All time is playtime.***

Try another idea...

The British artist and musician Bill Drummond also likes to play with these ideas (you can check his work out at www.penkiln-burn.com). He once planned a tour for the band Echo & the Bunnymen based on the idea that their route would draw out a giant pair of bunny ears across the map of the UK.

Another group of artists, the Boyle family, threw darts randomly at a map of the world and have been travelling to these places ever since, taking photographs of the corresponding portion of land – be it pavement, wasteland or beach – and then creating an exact replica of it from resin and fibreglass.

'So you see, imagination needs noodling – long, inefficient, happy idling, dawdling and puttering.'
BRENDA UELAND, writer

Defining idea...

We're not expecting you to go that far, but you could try a different kind of journey around your home, following a trail that's based not on a normal function (e.g. 'I need to brush my teeth so I'm going to the bathroom') but on some other sense of direction. For example, get hold of an audiotape guide of a gallery or your local town and use it to tour your home: 'In front of you is a marvellous sculpture from the nineteenth century,' says the tape, while you're stood in front of your TV in the living room. 'Turn left and enter a beautiful park,' says the tape. You turn left and you're in the downstairs toilet. This should help you look at your world in a very different way and make connections between different geographical spaces.

Alternatively, you could make your own audiotapes that describe a favourite walk in general terms and then apply it to other walks in places you don't really like.

Scott Paterson has been experimenting for a number of years with ideas about using mobile technologies to map out big cities in terms of personal experience and emotional reactions – rather than just checking off where the nearest shoe-store is. Check it out at www.pdpal.com

Q   **What's with all this wandering? I got lost and it took ages to get home.**

How did it go?

A   *If all you were worried about was knowing where you were and how you might get home, you weren't really entering into the spirit of the exercise. The whole point is to drift aimlessly so that you don't care about where you're going or where you're going to end up.*

Q   **It's not easy finding time to go 'deriving'. Is there a short-cut I could take?**

A   *This is always going to be a problem for would-be creative people who have jobs to do and families to go home to. Perhaps you could confine yourself to a short dérive for just an hour, say, in the park. If you can make time to go to the gym (or the pub), you've surely got time to have a go at this. Better still, get your mates or your family involved and all drift together. A family outing with no particular aim and no planning – now that's really flirting with danger!*

29

Familiar paths, tracks and runs

Change your journey to work, go home a different way – or don't go home at all.

You now know all about wandering off the beaten track. This time, think about different ways of completing journeys you've taken many times before.

Many of us have rat-runs and desire paths that we follow every day without really thinking about it. If you're a regular commuter to and from work, you'll know all about this. And quite often it feels like you're operating on autopilot. You know the best route to the train station, you know exactly what time you'll arrive at work to the nearest 30 seconds, you know already which coffee shop or café you're going to stop in at on the way. This is not good for a creative person – in fact, it's like the creative equivalent of anti-matter. So you should always be looking for ways of disrupting your routine, and therefore jerking yourself out of your habitual thought patterns.

Here's an idea for you...

Go up to various people and ask them for directions to the same place. Note how each person has a different way of describing the same route, focusing on different landmarks and shortcuts. How does the way they see things compare with your own?

The simplest way to make a familiar route a bit strange would be to travel it by means of another mode of transport. Instead of driving, take the train; instead of the train, take a bus; instead of a bus, ride a bike. Or maybe you should cut to the chase and just run to work.

Try also to mix up the media that you associate with different modes of transport. For example, a lot of people read newspapers on the train and not a lot of chatting goes on. On a bus, chatting is very much allowed (why, we don't know) and there's a lot more staring out of the window. In cars, there's a lot of staring out of windows, but reading newspapers is generally regarded as a bad idea, especially if you're driving. If you're travelling underground, mobile phone conversations are nixed and space is confined, so often people read paperback books or listen to personal hi-fis. These are all things to notice and react against. Try chatting on the train and staring out of the window on the underground.

All the little rituals of a typical journey also require your scrutiny. Why do you always buy the same coffee from the same vendor, or always read the same kind of book by the same kind of author? Why do you always buy the local newspaper on the way back from work, but never on the way there (OK, we admit there might be a good reason for that one)?

Defining idea...

'Be like the fox who makes more tracks than necessary, some in the wrong direction.'
WENDELL BERRY, farmer and writer

Check out other people's rituals too. If you haven't noticed already, there's a whole load of other people travelling along the same paths as you. What do they get up to? What are they doing with their journey time? What are their habits? Make notes. Maybe go as far as writing down the times that all your 'regulars' appear and disappear. They will become characters. Tiny fluctuations in their habits will form big significances in your mind. You can invent reasons for changes in their travel times, general behaviour, hairstyles, and before you know it, you've got yourself a story. As long as you're not intrusive, you could even play at surreptitiously following them. Follow, say, a person with red clothing until you come across another, then jump from person to person. There are some great movies that concentrate on this idea – Richard Linklater's *Slacker*, Robert Altman's *Short Cuts* and Tarkovsky's *Stalker*. If this sounds a bit creepy, well, hell, that's because it is. People watching can be creepy, especially if it veers into stalking – so please be careful out there, and do respect other people's privacy and personal space.

Try to make your approach to routine stuff more playful. IDEA 22, *All time is playtime*, suggests more ways.

Try another idea...

'The creative approach, the right approach, is deceptively simple: avoid the commonplace; try something different. Trying change for the sake of change isn't a meaningless exercise for the creative person; it's a systematic method for achieving better results.'
MARTIN HOLLOWAY, designer

Defining idea...

129

How did it go?

Q **Are there some ways of doing this kind of thing without looking like a loon or a weirdo?**

A *In Mark Haddon's novel* The Curious Incident of the Dog in the Night-time *his central character describes a way of locating a place by spiralling in on it via a series of left turns. Try doing only left turns on your next journey. Nobody else will notice (unless, of course, they're following you), but it will be a mental challenge for you. Alternatively, try not walking on the cracks in the pavement. Tim's personal favourite is to pace his journeys so that he reaches every pedestrian signal just as the 'Walk' sign is lighting up. Having to slow up or accelerate would look odd if he hadn't become expert at suddenly stopping and pretending to take an interest in something trivial – or suddenly looking like he's just remembered the time and is late. Throughout, Tim is fully concentrating, play-acting and disciplining his behaviour while very much living 'in the now' – all good things for a creative person to be doing. (He doesn't do this every day.)*

Q **I got lost and was late for work. Is this going to happen every time?**

A *Well, it is true that many a fell-walker has mistakenly taken a path that was made by sheep not humans and ended up in a field at the top of the mountain where the grass is tasty, rather than in the pub. But do bear in mind that you are supposed to be getting from A to B in a prescribed time – just in a different way.*

30

Genius on the go

Nature is creating all the time, everywhere. So take the hint, and use the back of a cab, the bus stop and the airport lounges as your studio.

Some years ago, the famous arts curator Hans Ulrich Obrist organised a conference with all of the usual infrastructure — the parties, the chats, the lunches, the airport arrivals — but no actual conference.

Apparently it was hugely successful and spawned many ongoing collaborations.

Apart from proving the point that informal networking can be very productive, Obrist's conference also shows that there are spaces beyond and between our traditional workplaces where it is still possible to get work done.

Here's an
idea for
you...

Go to the airport when you don't have a flight to catch. Airports are amazing places, full of people in transit from all parts of the globe, many of them having just arrived from a different time zone so that even the concept of night and day has been muddled up. The really big airports never actually sleep, so the middle of the night is a good time to just hang out there. Instead of a traveller passing through, think of yourself as a citizen of the airport, settle in for a few hours and start doing some work.

By setting up shop, as it were, in unfamiliar places you are far more likely to meet new, unfamiliar people and pick up on the kind of creative stimuli you couldn't hope to find in your normal studio or office. The easiest way to start feeding off this idea is to identify and spend time in the places you normally just pass through. Similarly, you should strive to be productive in the places where you usually just wait and 'kill time'.

Of course, advances in mobile technology mean that we can get a lot more done on the move these days. It's clear, though, that in many cases we use this technology to do extra layers of quite meaningless communication, such as telling our loved ones that 'we're on the train', reorganising files pointlessly or drafting an email that we otherwise wouldn't have bothered writing at all.

Be careful you don't use your mobile phone as the means for actually avoiding any real sense of belonging with the space you have chosen to occupy. The most creative communication you can have in the back of a cab, for example, is usually with the cab driver, not with anyone on the phone. And part of the point of occupying transitory and 'interstitial' spaces is precisely to put yourself in the way of a new and unusual interactions, not to simply replicate the processes that go on at home or in the office.

Part of this business of getting out into the world is very much about making yourself available to strangers (but not in any dodgy way, you understand.) At the bus stop and on the bus, switch off the mobile phone maybe and tune in instead to your surroundings: look out of the window, survey the scene, eavesdrop on the conversations of other passengers, talk to your neighbour.

We've already warned you to use mobile technology with discretion. But use it you probably will. So why not visit IDEA 46, *Tools of the trade – technology?*

Try another idea...

If you're not very good at talking to strangers, practice more and create situations where you have no choice but to talk. Ask directions, ask the time, ask when the next bus is due – ask anything that might lead to a new and interesting encounter. Don't worry if the interaction is short and cursory. Like the buses themselves, another one will be along any minute.

If you work from home and don't have a call to use public transport, there are still many interstitial spaces available to work in. There's the garden, the kitchen, your front door, the park, the local playground, the school gate, the corner shop, the pub, the postbox, the car, the neighbour's fence...we could go on.

'When I am, as it were, completely myself, entirely alone, and of good cheer – say, travelling in a carriage or walking after a good meal – it is on such occasions that my ideas flow best and most abundantly.'
WOLFGANG AMADEUS MOZART

Defining idea...

How did
it go?

Q My work is all about teamwork. How can I be good at this if I'm always on the move or sitting at a bus stop?

A   *You could always arrange to meet your team in these interstitial spaces instead of meeting over coffee or round a desk. Try a bus stop or in the back of a cab. Or choose a tourist spot or an eye-catching monument. If all the meeting requires is a bit of chat and informal note-taking, why not do it while walking round an art gallery or exercising the dog?*

Q I'm too shy to spend a lot of time in public spaces as you suggest. Do I have to do it?

A   *What do you think will happen to you if you start talking to strangers in public places? Do you think they'll be rude or laugh at you? Honestly, most people are incredibly friendly, helpful and sociable, and are probably as nervous as you are about striking up a conversation. As long as you're open and polite, nothing but good should come from extending your social skills.*

Q I like to keep work and play neatly separated. It helps me relax. Do I have to lose that?

A   *There is a case for saying that these interim spaces we've been talking about only excite us precisely because they provide a buffer zone between critical areas of our life. All the more reason, we say, to spend time there, so you have some kind of neutral zone in which to explore what would happen to you if things started to blur.*

31

The love of loneliness

Is working in isolation really good for you? Or would you be better off hosting a thousand golden daffodils?

So who's right here? Kafka or Miller? Do you need quiet solitude or a rollicking good party in order to be creative?

The romantic tradition of the solitary artist 'wandering lonely as a cloud' is still remarkably strong even today, despite the fact that many modern creative people do actually feed off the company of others.

Many of us survive intellectually thanks to a wealth of external stimuli and information sources that we'd never engage with if we were locked up in a garret in the middle of nowhere. You're reading a classic example of a project that couldn't have been written if either Rob or Tim had decided to retire to a country retreat in order to complete their half of the work alone. Having said that, many of our best ideas have come in workshops that have taken place in country barns, mountain hideaways and royal salt mines (we kid you not – not even about the royal bit). So getting away from it all clearly has some benefits.

Here's an idea for you... **Observe your own version of the Sabbath. It's increasingly trendy these days to take a 'data sabbath': one day a week turn off all electronic devices, avoid the TV and the radio, don't answer the phone and resist the urge to check your email.**

So what are those benefits? Well, for a start, getting away from the hustle and bustle of normal life definitely gives you time to concentrate and frees you from distractions. If you're not someone who is good at maintaining focus, then going to a place where there is nothing to focus on except the work in hand is going to be a good thing.

However, choosing a location with poor communications to the outside world (say, a place where mobile phones won't work and it's a couple of miles to the nearest shop) can be a double-edged sword. Sure, it's good to limit the capacity for interruptions, but it's a little less desirable if you have to walk half a mile up a hill in order to say goodnight to your kids on the phone.

Seeking solitude abroad isn't always everything it's cracked up to be, either. Going somewhere where you don't speak the language can be a great way of cutting yourself off. However, if you're in need of a doctor, say, having drunk the local water because you couldn't afford the time or interruption involved in visiting the nearest shop 3 km away, or you just want to know where the nearest restaurant is, it can be a case of cutting your nose off to spite your face.

Defining idea... **'Be quite still and solitary. The world will freely offer itself to you to be unmasked. It has no choice. It will roll in ecstasy at your feet.'**
FRANZ KAFKA

So: if you're convinced that exiling yourself to the back of beyond is really going to do you some good (and you can tell we're not convinced), do make sure that you pack a few creature comforts. Take plenty of 'kit' with you: your basic tools, plus cameras, pens, stationery, printers and so on. And take plenty of books, CDs, DVDs and whatever else is going to keep you entertained during those long evenings when there's absolutely nothing to do. On the other hand, you could follow Henry Miller's advice and organise an all-night party...

Cutting yourself off in a place where such things as food, drink and laundry have all been sorted for you will obviously make it easier for you to get down to some work. But according to IDEA 51, *Distraction loops*, those little chores may well have been providing you with the breaks from creative work that you sometimes need.

Try another idea...

If you've only got a limited amount of time away, there's no point coming back absolutely knackered because you've been working solidly. You still need to create some structure in the day and make sure this includes plenty of extracurricular activity. (A tour of the attic to see the bat shit springs to mind. Or a tour of an abandoned mine dressed in weird purple gowns led by a robot. These are two activities Rob and Tim have personally enjoyed during memorable creative retreats.)

'Develop interest in life as you see it; in people, things, literature, music – the world is so rich, simply throbbing with rich treasures, beautiful souls and interesting people. Forget yourself.'
HENRY MILLER

Defining idea...

How did it go?

Q   **Do I have to go into retreat all alone or can I take a friend?**

A   *So just how close is this friend? And what kind of creative work are you going to do together? Seriously, you probably don't want people around all the time if you're trying to work in peace. On the other hand, it's good to accept visitors – especially if they can provide some insight into what you're trying to achieve or give you a critique of your work. Every time you go away, you must set a deadline, or more importantly a target for what you want to achieve. Having someone around to whom you can be accountable is always going to be helpful.*

Q   **It's difficult enough to clear my desk for holidays, let alone a creative retreat. Can I leave it for when I get back?**

A   *One important aspect of setting off 'in retreat' is to make effective use of the time before going away. We always find that going on a trip forces us into getting a whole bunch of things done (consolidating notes, organising, backing up, tidying up, etc.). Quite often you start getting things done that otherwise would have hung around for weeks. Organising a retreat therefore could teach you how to make more space for holidays too.*

32

Travelogues, travelblogs

How to (b)log your travels (and travails) in a useful and entertaining way. Share and compare your blog with others – have a blog jam.

Ever since you were at school you've been asked to write about what you did on your holidays. Noting down your experiences of travel will always provoke interesting thoughts, and provide you with lots of creative research material.

It will also help you remember things that might otherwise get forgotten in the mists of time.

Quite how you share those thoughts and travel notes is another matter. We are not all born travel writers. On the other hand, stringing together an entertaining travelogue can be a great way to dip a toe into the difficult waters of storytelling and structuring a creative presentation of your work. This could be as corny as putting on a slideshow of holiday snaps for the neighbours once a year. Or it could be rigorously keeping a daily diary of all your wanderings – both offline and online.

Here's an idea for you... **Google 'Jill Walker blogging' and you'll find a really good definition of what blogging is. New media academic Jill Walker also has some interesting things to say about how writing in a network can fundamentally change the way you think about writing.**

Online travelogues of various descriptions are becoming incredibly popular, and the most pervasive form of this at the moment is weblogging, or 'blogging'. Blogging started as a very simple concept. You keep a 'log' of your 'web' activity – where you've been, whom you've met, plus your thoughts and reactions – and then you publish it as a series of links and comments, for others to read and use as a customised and topical snapshot of current web activity.

The new generation of personal publishing software from companies such as Google and Six Apart has meant that budding bloggers require very little knowledge of HTML programming or web design in order to get going. Changes and updates can be completed rapidly and frequently, so blog sites can react to events with amazing speed.

Blogs are also very easy to find, since the other distinguishing aspect of the software is the number of ways that are provided to link to other blogs, be alerted to blog site updates, syndicate your own blog and generally promote yourself within the blogging community.

Defining idea... *'Like all great travellers, I have seen more than I remember, and remember more than I have seen.'* BENJAMIN DISRAELI

People can then follow the same creative trail as you, and you have something to refer back to and make sense of. It's very easy and inexpensive to start a blog. Check out www.blogger.com or www.typepad.com.

There are two basic reasons for wanting to log your online adventures:

1. ARCHIVING

Elsewhere we've mentioned the importance of keeping a record as you go of your experiences, thoughts and ideas – so you can refer back to them for later use. The immediacy and ease with which you can record your thoughts and feelings means there's no good excuse not to. Sure, you can do this with your fancy Moleskin notepad or a tape recorder or a camera, but by doing it all on the Web and uploading everything to a remote server, you have the peace of mind of knowing it's backed up and hard to lose. Nobody we know has yet made a back up of their Moleskin. Also, typing on a keyboard into a limited frame concentrates the mind wonderfully and stops you from rambling. Because of the restrictions of time and space, you learn quickly only to record and tag the good stuff.

> **Even the seemingly mundane journeys you take every day could be worth logging. See how in IDEA 29, *Familiar paths, tracks and runs*.**

Try another idea...

2. SHARING

Producing a travelogue is not just for your own benefit. It's good to share your journey with others. Not only does this sense of a readership or viewing audience make you think carefully about how you present your work, there's also the potential – via comments and emails – for feedback. Each member of your audience is a traveller too and may well have stories to tell about travelling down the same road you're currently treading. You want to be able to learn from their experience and benefit from their creative research as well as your own. So, wherever possible in your travelogue, allow space for people to respond to your work and also tie you into their travelogues too.

> **'Too often travel, instead of broadening the mind, merely lengthens the conversation.'**
> ELIZABETH DREW, author

Defining idea...

In blog terms, you need to 'think link' as much as possible.

How did it go?

Q **I'm too busy enjoying the journey to bother recording it. Why should I spoil it?**

A Sometimes it's important to just be in and of the moment. You don't want to be one of those people on holiday who see everything through a lens. Maybe the best strategy is to combine online and offline logging. Keep a notebook handy and in a quiet moment jot down what's happening, what you're thinking and feeling. Then summarise this later in a pithy blog entry. Many people write their daily diaries at the end of the day rather than during it – do the same with your blog.

Q **Writing down 'what I did on my holiday' is all a bit cheesy, isn't it?**

A Don't get bogged down by the minutiae or think of this as some kind of banal postcard you're sending home to mum. Think of your (potential) audience. What is it about your day that would be useful for us all to know? What bits of it do you really think are worth saving for posterity?

Q **Isn't it expensive and complicated to set up a blog?**

A No. It's really easy and cheap. You shouldn't need to spend more than a few bucks a month on server space and you can rely on basic design templates to start with that require little or no configuration on your part. Most big blogging companies offer a thirty-day free trial anyway, so you don't need to part with any cash at all up front.

33

Creative tourism

The alternative guide to being abroad – because being on holiday doesn't mean taking a break from creativity.

Most of us when we go on holiday generate a huge amount of creative output in a very short space of time — often without even noticing it.

Not only do you have to put a lot of thought and energy into planning your holiday and getting to your chosen destination, once you're there you pass much of the time doing things an artist would do: taking photos, shooting video, writing (postcards), assembling items (souvenirs) into tableaux and thinking about your audience. (Who will you write to? Who will you buy presents for?)

In your spare time – if you have any – you'll also be immersing yourself in other forms of culture: trying the food, seeing the sights, mastering the language, learning about the local history. When you list out all the creative things you do on holiday like this, it's a wonder that you don't come back completely exhausted.

Here's an idea for you...

In the work *45 Postkarten aus Berlin* artist Kirsten Pieroth sent unwritten postcards found in Berlin thrift stores back to their origin. Each was sent to the specific place depicted on the front of the card (Google 'Pieroth Postkarten' and you'll find more details) and the recipients were asked to write back saying what that place was really like. Try this yourself. Send a postcard of Buckingham Palace to the Queen and ask her to write back!

Since these times of your life are clearly fantastic opportunities to stretch your wings, we've got a few ideas about others ways you could be creative with vacation paraphernalia.

POSTCARDS

Postcards seem to hold a certain fascination for artists. Joseph Beuys, for example, used to make all sort of postcards out of wood or vinyl, and sometimes even magnetic or sulphurous ones. As an interesting exercise, on your next holiday don't confine yourself to the postcards that you can buy in the shops, but dream up ones of your own. Challenge yourself, even, about what can be called a postcard and still be delivered in the postal system for the price of one stamp.

PHOTOS

It's almost unthinkable to go on holiday without a camera these days. Do you want the anticipation of celluloid, or instant digital gratification?

LOCATIONS

Trendy guidebooks always tell you to avoid the usual places where tourists go to get off the beaten track. But we say, go to the popular places and think about ways to reinvigorate familiar sights. What could you do, for example, to make a visit to the Eiffel Tower different from the norm? (Avoid queuing, for a start.)

If your perfect holiday is all about doing nothing, we have some tips about that too, in IDEA 52, *Do absolutely nothing.*

Try another idea...

VIDEOS

Wherever we go in the world nowadays there always seems to be someone with a handicam. Quite often the footage that ends up being taken is of 'views' that would be better captured with a good stills camera, or group shots of people waving (good-bye or hello? Or 'look behind you'?) – or of kids running about, falling over or eating food in a humorous way. If you get hold of one of these cameras, always try to plan out what your going to shoot as if it's a pseudo-documentary, an interview or a drama.

Treat travel as an opportunity to use new locations for projects that you couldn't hope to film at home. And always experiment with the functions on your camera. If your model allows you to film in the dark using nightvision, find an excuse to do it.

'The bandwidth of the world is greater than that of your TV set, or the Internet, or even a totally immersive, interactive, dynamically rendered, object-oriented, real-time graphic-simulated computer experience.'
BRUCE MAU, designer

Defining idea...

SOUNDS

Ambient sound is one of the most underrated sources of inspiration in our world, and by travelling you have the opportunity to collect an amazing array of exotic noises and unusual fragments of speech. Sometimes a tape recorder is a better thing to take on holiday than a camera (though not as good as a towel).

SOUVENIRS

Souvenir shops are very strange places, full of stuff that you wouldn't buy at home in a month of Sundays and doesn't appear to have any use in this world. Think, then – if you wanted to sell souvenirs to people who visited your home or your place of work, what would be in your shop?

Q   **I've never had the opportunity to travel abroad. How am I to broaden my perceptual horizons?**

A   There's a fine tradition of sending postcards, buying souvenirs and travelling without leaving home on the Web. Your authors, Rob and Tim, are specialists in this, in fact. Take a holiday today on our imaginary Greek island Mount Kristos (www.mountkristos.com), or send a virtual gift via www.it3c.co.uk. If you want to help build an imaginary town out of postcards, souvenirs and memories, come to Oldton (www.oldton.com).

Q   **My holidays are about going to the middle of nowhere with none of the kit you describe in this section. How can I play?**

A   What? Not even some paper and a pen? We don't believe you. Surely it would be nice to capture those feelings of oneness with nature and being at peace with the world in some way that would allow you to revisit or reclaim those feelings at a later date? Have you ever thought of writing poetry, for example? Or if you're really stuck, try knitting about your experience or scratching some notes on your arm with a bramble.

How did it go?

149

34

Network near, network far

Learn to value friends – and appreciate enemies.

Did you know that people who fail to keep up a good number of friendships into their middle age and beyond are less likely to live as long as the rest of us?

It's official – having a wide network of people to talk to is good for your health. Japanese health experts claim that regular face-to-face contact with friends and neighbours reduces stress and thus lowers the risk of stress-related illnesses.

In the UK, recent research suggested that middle-aged men in particular are prone to becoming too solitary (in their sheds, presumably) and thus shortening their life expectancy. Statistically, it has been known for years that married men – in social family environments – live longer than bachelors. All this goes to prove that putting yourself about a bit, making sure you're achieving a high turnover of new acquaintances, will help you to be not only more creative, but more healthy with it!

Most of us have surprisingly few genuine friends. Sure, your address book and your email client may be stacked full of names, but how many of them are really friends?

Here's an idea for you...

As well as playing games of 'Six Degrees of Separation', trying to connect two random people together based on who they know, why not indulge in a game of 'Six Degrees of Kevin Bacon', the game where you connect actors via films starring Kevin Bacon. Full rules at www.louisville.com/loumag/mar /bacon.htm

A BBC online survey revealed that on average people tended to have twenty friends in their address book, while during the week they only kept in contact with four to seven of these. (By the way, there was no significant difference between the figures for men and women.)

It's actually easier than ever to increase your circle of friends and acquaintances now that we live in a networked world, just by using your email. Go through your email inbox right now (assuming you have one – if you don't, sort it!). Perhaps you've already noticed how many times emails addressed to you have also been cc-ed to other people. Now ask yourself – how many people on that cc-list have you communicated with in a meaningful way? Not that many, we'd wager. Well now's the time to start.

Don't worry, this isn't what they call 'spamming' because you've already been connected to these seeming strangers via a shared email. And this email also gives you something to talk about. So pick out someone you've never really talked to before and start an email correspondence. Start with a 'Don't I know you?' query or a 'Can you help me?' request, or similar. Keep it light, be helpful and friendly, don't be bothersome, and make yourself look like you're someone useful to know. Stay alert to replies and slowly build up a rapport.

Why do this? Well, any new contact you make will expand your knowledge of the world at large and could lead to new ideas or collaborations. According to the theory of 'six degrees of separation' (whereby any two people in the world can be connected via a chain of aquaintances that is never longer than six people), by making contact with just a few people in this way, you'll be getting yourself hooked into a much larger social network very quickly indeed.

If you find someone famous and talented on your network who you'd really like to work with, what do you do? Go to IDEA 36, *Wanna work with the rich and famous? Just ask.*

Try another idea...

As internet commentator and social software academic Clay Shirky points out:

'The social tools of the internet, lightweight though most of them are, have a kind of fluidity and ease of use that the conference call never attained: compare the effortlessness of cc:ing half a dozen friends to decide on a movie, versus trying to set up a conference call to accomplish the same task.'

Exploiting and managing your network in this way can also mean you stay alert for people who really don't like you or your work. 'Keep your friends close, and your enemies closer,' advised Machiavelli (not to us personally, you understand). The good news is that on a well-run network you can see exactly what those bastards are up to (they're usually pretty vocal) and you can pre-empt every possible criticism of your creative endeavour well before it actually happens.

'My father said to me, many years ago, "Hang out with people who are brighter and smarter than you and they'll drag you up with them," and that has actually been the truth.'
MICHAEL PATRICK CRONAN, designer

Defining idea...

153

How did
it go?

Q **I'm always a bit nervous about meeting people – even online.
How can I overcome my natural shyness?**

A   *Being online can really help with this. We know a lot of people who are very
quiet and shy in real life, but who become positively noisy in a chat room or
on a forum. Get yourself a chat ID and try it. In the real world, a good
solution is to always share taxis or car-rides with other people, even if you
don't know them very well. You'll have to make some kind of light
conversation – and also you'll cut down on your transport costs. Just make
sure you're both going the same way.*

Q **Am I going to make meaningful contacts via online networks? People
who want to be friends with everyone are shallow, aren't they?**

A   *We're not saying you need to be friends with everyone, you just need to
extend your network. Think of developing new acquaintances for your
network as you might think of developing ideas. Some ideas require effort.
Some ideas just happen. Some last a long time and you have an intense
relationship with them. Others go on the back-burner or get rejected. It
doesn't mean you don't have respect for all of them. It doesn't mean either
that you have to live with all of them forever.*

35

Know what you can't do

Ferret out those failings and look for your limitations if you want to be free to focus on your strengths.

It can be curiously liberating to 'fess up to what you are crap at. There's a real tendency among creative people to control every aspect of their work. But work can suffer as a result.

It seems obvious to say that you shouldn't try to do everything yourself. But if you feel like you're just not getting any support from anywhere else, or that nobody else really understands what you're trying to do or you don't trust anyone to do what you want well enough, it's really tempting to go it alone.

The problem is that it is given to very few of us – if any at all – to be great at everything. If nothing else, there just isn't enough time in your life to be trained up with all the expertise you would need to be great at everything.

Here's an idea for you...

Corporations have lots of tools (personality tests, etc.) to identify basic personality types and assess potential employees in order to build teams. Adopt the same techniques (ironically if you must) to understand more about yourself. Online tests abound for you to play with (check out the sites www.personalitytype.com and www.humanmetrics.com). Use these to add to your strengths and weaknesses list.

We are all, to a greater or less extent, specialists. Perhaps you've never thought about yourself in that way. Perhaps now you should. The easy way to understand what your specialities are is to list them. Is there some aspect of your creativity that you draw upon more than any other? Is there a particular facility you have that makes you and your work stand out from the crowd? Is there some area of expertise that you are always consulted upon by others? Have you won prizes or awards for something special? Have your peers or your audience fed back particular things they like about you or your work?

On a more general level, you should be clear with yourself about both what you're good at – and what you're bad at. So go on, write out in detail all your strengths and weaknesses.

Defining idea...

'It's a wrong idea that a master is a finished person. Masters are very faulty; they haven't learned everything and they know it.'
ROBERT HENRI, artist

Admitting that you are bad at something isn't as easy as it sounds. OK, you can say 'I'm crap at drawing' and almost feel you mean it. But then if someone else says 'Yeah, you really are crap at drawing', your natural response is probably going to be 'Yeah, well, I'm not *that* bad'. This is the state of mind that leads you into not asking for help with drawing tasks from someone who is clearly a better draughtsperson than you.

As well as being brutal with yourself about what skills you really do lack, add to the list all the things you actually don't like doing. Chances are that if you don't get any joy out of doing something, you won't be much good at it either. Think of how kids get out of doing the washing up after dinner by pretending to be crap at it (partners too, come to think of it).

Let's be clear here: we're not talking just about practical things, such as writing or drawing or composing music (or washing up). We also want you to consider more fundamental things that relate to your personality type. Are you a social person? Bad tempered? Analytical? Impulsive? Conventional?

By now your list should be getting long. Don't get depressed. All it really shows you is that maybe you really do need to start collaborating more closely with a whole host of other people if you want your creative ideas to fly. Let them get on with the (in your eyes) dross while you concentrate on doing the important things.

Implicit in 'how to look for the things you lack' is how to find people who can do the things you can't. Discover how in IDEA 36, *Wanna work with the rich and famous? Just ask.*

Try another idea...

> *'We do not know one millionth of one percent about anything.'*
> THOMAS EDISON

Defining idea...

How did it go?

Q I wrote a list of all the things I can't do and it made me depressed. What hope have I got?

A *Think of this as a liberating process rather than anything designed to humiliate you or knock you down. Don't say 'I'm so useless I can't do any of this stuff' but rather, 'I don't need to waste my time with this stuff again, I'll find someone to help me'. You define yourself by what you can't do as much as by what you can. Every realisation about who you are and what you can and can't do is a step forward – so accept it and move on. And don't be judgemental either. Nothing about you is good or bad for your creativity per se. Besides, at least now you know you're good at making lists.*

Q I'm already well aware of my limitations, so this exercise didn't throw up any surprises. Haven't I just wasted my time?

A *Have you asked anyone else's opinion about this? We are often so wrapped up in ourselves that it's hard to see clearly what we're really like. Often, people with particularly strong personalities are the last to know about something that other people are well aware of. You might, for example, be labouring under the illusion that you're a good strategic thinker when everyone around you has known for years that you're useless. Try and find a time and place when someone else can tell you honestly what they think you're like. If nobody wants to talk to you about this, perhaps you should saddle up and go and see a therapist.*

36

Wanna work with the rich and famous? Just ask

If you want to give your project a boost, get some really talented people to work with you. All you've got to do is learn how to convince them.

One great way of fine-tuning your own creativity is to work alongside the talents of others. Paying people to work on your projects is the most obvious way to build a team.

But there are some people in the world who you'd like to work with who aren't really interested in the money. Some of them are interested in what they might learn rather than what they might earn from doing the work. Others might be turned on by the type of work you're offering, or the audience you're reaching with your work, or the social network that you're creating.

Here's an idea for you...

Research the person or people you're contacting. But at all costs, avoid coming over as an obsessive fan. Make it clear that you understand very well how and why their work will fit in with your aims. If possible, take a piece of their creative work and demonstrate how it fits in with your vision. If you're talking to a musician, for example, use their music as the soundtrack for your presentation.

Some people are just out of your league – too successful or famous already to bother stooping to your level. Rob (one of the authors, if you've forgotten) has a theory that the toughest people to get on your project are those with a single name, because it's such a mark of their own 'brand' success (think Madonna, think Spielberg, think Rob…OK, so we're still working on that last one).

But there's absolutely nothing to stop you asking someone incredibly famous to work with you if you genuinely think that the collaboration might be fruitful for you both. During their time together, Rob and Tim have approached a number of eminent people to work on projects and in many cases the response has been very positive. This shouldn't really be a surprise, since famous people are still creative individuals like you and are attracted to good ideas. Even on the occasions when the answer has been 'no' (as was the case with Harrison Ford, despite his having two names), the process of preparing materials for potential meetings gave the project concerned real impetus.

The principle in all this is obvious: the people you really want to work with might not be as busy, famous, successful or unapproachable as they might seem. So you may as well ask. The real challenge is to know how to ask in the right way.

Celebrities, for example, don't appreciate being approached via a home or email address that you've picked up on a stalker's website (as Tim will tell you from his bitter experience with Supertramp…). Sometimes, if you've built up a wide professional network, you may well have got hold of an email address via legitimate means. In which case, feel free to use it. But ensure that you write something concise and to the point, and which you intend to follow up with more formal communication.

Getting people interested in your ideas often requires a lot of talking from you. But it can be just as important to sit back and listen to them occasionally. See how in IDEA 37, *Lie back and listen*.

Try another idea…

Generally, if you're dealing with someone who is already successful you may well have to approach them via an agent, a PA (that's the personal assistant type, not the megaphone/loudspeakers variant, though that might be worth a go, too!), a production company or some form of business representative. Naturally this means that you're in danger of being fobbed off by flunkies and people who are actually paid to get rid of people like you. In which case, it will be your track record for getting good things done, allied to the quality of your current proposition and the materials you show to back up that concept, that will get you a foot in the door.

In terms of the materials that you generate in order to spark interest, always bear in mind that anyone creative looking from the outside is going to be asking the question: 'What's in it for me?' The bottom line is, if you can't make it clear why you see value in working together, the other person won't see it either.

'The only dumb question is the question that you don't ask.'
PAUL MacCREADY, inventor

Defining idea…

161

How did it go?

Q   **I asked and they said no. So what's the next step?**

A   *Never mind. If you managed to package your idea to the point where you could explain it to someone else and ask for their help, it means you've almost certainly progressed the idea quite substantially. One very good tip is that if someone turns you down, ask them if they know anyone else who might be interested. Always use this negative encounter to lead you on to a positive one. Help comes in many forms, by the way. You may have been looking for someone to put some hours in on production. But instead, maybe this person would be willing to publicly endorse what you're doing, or lead you to sources of funding.*

Q   **I've been asked if I want to work with someone else, but that would mean abandoning my own project. What should I do?**

A   *This happens a lot. You walk into a room hoping everyone is going to buy into your thing, and in fact the agenda is to try and employ your talent on their thing. Your creative work is a showcase for your talent, and it's just possible that your talent may be more marketable than your work. The calculation you need to make is whether by sacrificing some time now to work on something else, you will end up winning friends and support for your work in the end.*

37

Lie back and listen

Being passive can be part of the creative process too.

Just because you're not doing or saying something clever right now doesn't mean you're not helping.

If you're working in a creative team, it's important that you take you're turn at being the listener, because everybody likes (or needs) to be listened to at some point. Everyone needs a sounding board. The problem is that many creative environments are so packed with feisty, opinionated, creative people creating 'white noise' and general interference that sounding boards just don't work. It's important, therefore, to support a 'culture of listening' that encourages people to work through problems without interruption and propose solutions out loud before everyone else piles in with their own views and nuggets of homespun advice. Frankly, if you do your fair share of listening, you're much more likely to be listened to yourself when the time comes. And other team members are more likely to buy into this process if they feel they're being listened to (particularly by their superiors).

Listening is also about empathising with the talker – learning to see the world from their perspective. If you can develop this skill, you can get on with any of the people around you.

Here's an idea for you...

Note these top tips on how not to listen: (1) just keep talking; (2) when you're not talking, think about what you're going to say next; (3) interrupt frequently; (4) look away; (5) never, ever, ask clarifying questions. Courtesy of www.businesslistening.com

If you've got into a situation where you are required to listen more than you speak, there are some obvious pointers about how to be really effective.

■ Always let the other person finish making their points before you jump in. Even if you just want to agree or encourage, what you're doing is putting your ego first ('oh yes I agree...', 'the same thing happened to me...', etc.).

■ Don't try to 'fix' things too quickly. If the other person is voicing a problem, the first thing they want is your sympathy and support, so they can tackle their own problems with more confidence.

■ Don't give away your feelings about what you're hearing with loud sighs, snorts of derision or facial winces.

■ If you must talk, confine yourself at first to open questions that require something more than a yes and no. This will encourage the other person to say everything that needs to be said.

■ Don't bore them with stories of what you did or would have done in a similar situation.

Above all, try not to do anything else but listen. Don't use a computer, doodle, fidget or read something while someone else is talking to you. (Didn't your parents teach you anything?!) People will notice if you're not really paying attention and will be discouraged from speaking to you again. They'll also think you're bloody rude.

For your part, you'll be in danger of hearing only part of what is said, or worse, pretending to listen while you're actually thinking about something else. So minimise outside interruptions before starting an important listening session. Get rid of any background noise (like music playing), turn off your mobile phone and move to a more private space if necessary.

Sometimes the noise of other people can be horribly distracting and all you want to do is go somewhere far away, where it is peaceful and quiet – like IDEA 31, *The love of loneliness.*

Try another idea...

'I used to talk too much, but now I let the client do it all.'
ALEXANDER ISLEY, designer

Defining idea...

To test whether you really are listening or not, challenge yourself at the point that the other person has stopped speaking to recap the key points and sum up the emotional drift of the conversation in a few brief words ('so you're angry with Rob'). Doing this will clarify the value of what's just been said and deeply impress the other person with your listening skills.

Don't forget about body language too, such as eye contact, pauses and posture. Not only do you need to look interested – the general demeanour of the speaker might tell you a lot about what the real point of the conversation is. The first thing people bring up when they have something to say often isn't the central point they will eventually make. And sometimes the central point never gets made explicitly. Good listening can involve hearing what is *not* being said.

'We have two ears and one mouth so that we can listen twice as much as we speak.'
EPICTETUS

Defining idea...

165

How did
it go?

Q   The people I'm forced to listen to change their stories and ideas from week to week. What's the point of listening at all?

A   *Maybe you need to keep records of what's been said. If you've listened well and summarised accurately, keeping records should be easy – and that's going to make it more difficult for people to change their story further down the line. By 'minuting' creative meetings and maybe even outlining some kind of action plan that arises from them, there's less chance of miscommunication within the team. And you won't have to harbour feelings of resentment about people using you as some kind of passive listening post.*

Q   I'm such a great listener that I never get to speak! When's it my turn?

A   *Well, you can always listen to yourself. Seriously, it can be quite therapeutic to give yourself a good talking to. It gets stuff out of your system, and by articulating your thoughts and feelings you may well identify things about yourself that you hadn't seen before. The alternative is therapy.*

Q   Do I really have to listen to everything people want to tell me?

A   *No. If someone is wandering off the point or wasting your time, don't put up with it. Bring the conversation to a close (tactfully) and arrange a time to speak again when you feel you are in the mood to listen. Always, though, be honest with yourself about why you don't want to listen right now. It may actually be because something else is on your mind and nothing to do with the other person at all.*

38

Playing consequences

Pass ideas along a chain of people and see how the ideas change and combine as they go.

You must have played this game. Somebody draws a head, folds the paper and passes it on. The next person draws a body, folds and passes. The third person draws the legs. A strange collaborative beast is born.

Actually the version of the game that generates such a Frankensteinian monster is called 'The Exquisite Corpse', and was used a lot by key personalities within the surrealist movement, such as André Breton and Marcel Duchamp. They developed it as a method for assembling words into sentences at first, rather than using it for drawing pictures. The name 'exquisite corpse' came from a phrase that occurred when the game was first played in French: 'Le cadavre exquis boira du nouveau vin.' ('The exquisite corpse will drink the new wine.')

The basic idea of this kind of exercise is to get a group of people to write in sequence, with each person only seeing the end what the previous person wrote. Try it yourself with a group of friends and see what you come up with.

Here's an idea for you...

If you don't have anyone to collaborate/play games with, carry out your own acts of blind chance. The 'cut up' technique beloved of William Burroughs is a great way to spread disorder. Write out a seemingly normal sequence of text, then cut it up into single words or phrases. Now reassemble the pieces in any order. If you're a songwriter like David Bowie this technique can be a very handy way of coming up with 'discovered' lyrics that don't necessarily make full sense but go rather well with the music. At least we think that's the explanation for a song like *The Secret Life of Arabia*.

Defining idea...

'When the way comes to an end, then change – having changed, you pass through.'
From the *I Ching*

Only once have Rob and Tim managed to create a full-blown rhyming poem this way:

David Gower, David Gower
do you believe in
nuclear power?

It's not great, we know, but it demonstrates that something can emerge out of this process of working together partially in the dark.

Quite a lot of creative collaborations actually do work in this way. We know ours does sometimes. Since Rob is chiefly a designer and programmer and Tim is chiefly a writer, it is sometimes hard for either of them to really 'see' what the other is up to. Tim sends Rob scripts that his non-linear brain can't quite process. Rob sends Tim images and interactive sequences that just confuse the hell out of him. Nevertheless, we send each other documents and files that the other is meant to work from and hope that something strange and beautiful (or usually 'short, funny and clever', just as the client asked for) will eventually appear.

It's interesting, then, to think of all the creative output that you send to other people as just one 'turn' in a game of consequences, rather than a complete and whole piece of work that others should tamper with at their peril. This approach also lets you off the hook from thinking that you have to do it all, straight off the bat. Instead you could concentrate on offering a starting point only, with some kind of 'way in' for the next person, allowing them to continue where you left off. Alternatively you could think of simply leaving a blank space somewhere in your work for someone else to fill in.

There are in fact all manner of ways to allow for more of the unexpected, the random and the surreal in your work.

If you like playing consequences, there's a game called 'spitball' you might like, as explained in IDEA 40, *Spit it out*.

Try another idea...

'I used to think anyone doing anything weird was weird. Now I know that it is the people that call others weird that are weird.'
PAUL McCARTNEY

Defining idea...

171

Q **I don't like the randomness of the results in this game. How can I make it less wasteful?**

A *The randomness is usually just a function of how inventive and intuitive the players of the game turn out to be. If you try this kind of working method with the same people over a longer period of time, we think some kind of innate understanding will come into play that will more or less guarantee interesting results. Stick at it. Maybe it didn't feel right to be doing something where no single person could see the whole of the picture? An alternative is to adopt the method of 'Chinese whispers' instead, whereby the first person whispers a word or phrase into the second person's ear, who whispers what they think they heard into the third person's ear and so on. Working to this model, you know exactly what you started with and only you as the first player in the game can understand the distortions that have taken place.*

Q **I find when you play consequences, particularly with the same people, that a number of common themes or symbols tend to emerge. Is this a good or a bad thing?**

A *Good question. Why not try a couple of variations to find out? Make a list of your common themes and symbols, and then play the game choosing only from items on the list. Then play it again but this time ban them all. Which version was most successful? Chances are the 'restricted' version might produce more interesting results over time.*

39

Come the revolution! Toppling top dogs and overturning hierarchies

Everybody knows that tiered management is for faceless bean-counters while creative environments are shared, open, and free from rank and hierarchies. Sure as salmon live up trees and eat pencils.

Lots of creative types like to think they work in a cosy non-hierarchical environment where no one person is the boss, everyone has their say and there is 'shared ownership' of the project. In 99.99% of cases, this is delusional bullshit.

OK, if you work alone or are self-employed you will have more of a chance of being your own boss and working in an open culture of free exchange (with yourself, presumably). Having said that, some of the most right-wing megalomaniacs we ever

Here's an idea for you... **Create an informal system of people (colleagues, family?) taking turns to shoulder the blame for everything. If it is your day, then you have to apologise for everything from the weather, to running out of coffee, to missing that deadline. To find a little more about invisible hierarchies try it yourself – you may be surprised by who finds it funny and who doesn't cope so well.**

met were self-employed or lone workers who couldn't wait to boss other people about.

It's actually unproven that non-hierarchical structures lead to the most creative collaborations. Hives of industrial creativity, such as Disney or Dreamworks, or many of the world's large advertising agencies, have very clear and distinct lines of management and decision making – even if some of them adopt a load of wishy-washy New Age speak to try and convince you otherwise (check out www.stlukes.co.uk for a healthy dose of that.)

Readers of this book may well come from different strata of the creative hierarchy, and therefore will have different opinions about whether flattening the line of command, or even turning everything on its head, is a good idea.

What it all boils down to is the questioning of authority. And not just the authority of others, but also your own. Ask yourself: what gives you the right to make decisions, to be in charge, or even be creative?!

So how do you get the most out of the whole creative team?

IF YOU ARE A BOSS

If you're at the top of a creative organisation, it's about listening to the people below and then encouraging a culture of 'overturning'; that is, allowing those people to actually put their ideas into practice irrespective of their status within the organisation or on the team.

If you can't be the boss, at least find ways of sharing your ideas. See IDEA 45, *Give it all away.*

Try another idea...

IF YOU ARE A MANAGER

You need to think about changing the 'rules of engagement' in terms of how you organise teams and roles within teams. The rules that may have been successful in the past may no longer be applicable today. So be prepared to trash them and start again. Review the way things are being done as often as you can.

IF YOU ARE A WORKER

Sadly, if you're at the bottom it's very hard to overturn entrenched hierarchies, particularly at work. However, you can use brainstorming meetings and 'off-sites' to assert your independence, question current structures and generally have your own say. Just don't expect a particularly friendly reception from some of the managers! (Perhaps it's time you went freelance?!)

'If two or three persons should come with a high spiritual aim and with great powers, the world would fall into their hands like a ripe peach.'
RALPH WALDO EMERSON

Defining idea...

175

Defining idea...

'You do not lead by hitting people over the head. That's assault, not leadership.'
DWIGHT D. EISENHOWER

IF YOU ARE AN ADMINISTRATOR

You have the power to change quite a lot within a creative organisation, since changes in administrative systems can often lead to radical cultural change. For example, when the accountants decided it was a good idea to give journalists computers instead of typewriters, it shifted the balance of power away from sub-editors and typesetters and changed the newspaper industry forever.

IF YOU ARE A REBEL

Creative organisations will support arsey individuals indefinitely if they believe the individuals have talent (which explains the career of many a creative director within the ad agency business). But don't kick out just for the hell of it. Without a good reason for being bolshy, you'll run out of rope eventually.

IF YOU ARE A GOOSE

In the end, whatever your role, we suggest that you all try to act more like geese. Geese, when they fly south for the winter, do so in the well-known V formation. The fittest, strongest bird flies at the front of the V, taking the brunt of the weather and protecting the others in his slipstream. When this leader gets tired, another bird takes over. Throughout the flight, the geese will swap positions many times to help each other out. If one goose gets really tired, it'll land for a rest and join the next V formation that comes along.

Now that's a model for mutual support and non-hierarchical teamwork. And how do they establish this culture? With loud and frequent honking, of course!

So, if you really want to work in a flatter, more democratic environment with people you can respect as your peers, make sure that you make loud positive honks frequently about your state of health, your current location and your function within the group. Effective communication is the key.

Happy honking.

Q **We have very formal reporting structures in our workplace that we all have to stick to. Is this a problem?**

How did it go?

A *Structure can be good. And if the reporting is actually leading to good communication and useful documentation of your creative processes, then there isn't much to complain about. Perhaps the only concern might be when a bit of initiative needs to be taken quickly by someone at the coalface of an idea. If you're all waiting for the right moment to report a problem in the 'appropriate' way, nobody's ever going to seize the moment and light that creative spark.*

Q **We tried to let everyone have a go at being in charge, and anarchy ensued. Too many chefs and all that. Should we revert to the tried and tested?**

A *There are never too many chefs. You just need a bigger kitchen that's better organised and stocked with more high-quality ingredients. Also, chefs need to learn how to specialise (sauces, pastries, desserts, etc.) and know when to defer to the expertise of another.*

40

Spit it out

Why spitting in public may not be such a bad thing. Even over and over and over.

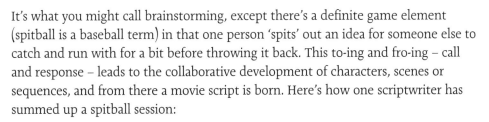

'Spitball' is a movie industry term to describe the process before a script has been written, when the writing team is just sitting around throwing ideas at each other.

It's what you might call brainstorming, except there's a definite game element (spitball is a baseball term) in that one person 'spits' out an idea for someone else to catch and run with for a bit before throwing it back. This to-ing and fro-ing – call and response – leads to the collaborative development of characters, scenes or sequences, and from there a movie script is born. Here's how one scriptwriter has summed up a spitball session:

'Usually we spitball every single idea, whether it be a small idea, or an entire scene, or a story...we don't really categorize them or judge them in any way. Literally we just take notes and notes, and usually go as broad and as far as we can. Then we write an extremely long vomit draft, as we like to call it, and then we keep whittling it away.'

Here's an idea for you...

In baseball, the term 'spitball' refers to a ball that has been tampered with by the application of spit, vaseline or another foreign substance before it is thrown. Think about this as you throw your ideas back and forth: make sure each time that you deliberately tamper with them by applying a little foreign substance.

Crucial to this idea of spitball is not only the tossing around of ideas and stories, but the preparedness of everyone concerned to tread the same ground again and again. Repetition is the key.

In the process of creative spitball, a character description or story is repeated by each person in turn as they catch the ball. This 'receiver' is then expected to polish the idea or put some kind of spin on it, then throw it on to the next person. The new receiver may remove some kind of blemish or reshape the idea a little before passing it on…

Retelling an idea back to each other over and over again is a fantastic way of picking at it, discovering its flaws and making refinements until you have something that really stands up in everybody's eyes.

Even if you don't have someone to play spitball with, you can still keep re-presenting your ideas to yourself each day. Whatever the weather and whatever your mood, go over it again. By doing so, some aspects of your idea will harden and others will weaken with wear. Perhaps you will start to get very slick in parts (perhaps too slick?). Tellingly, you'll probably also stutter and stumble over the same areas each time – areas that you feel unsure about or that require further thought and elaboration.

Defining idea...

'I love to spitball. You know, just sitting around, throwing out ideas.'
WILLIAM GOLDMAN, screenwriter

It's always better to involve other people in this process if you can. In fact, wherever and whenever you are given the opportunity, share your story. The reactions of different audiences can be invaluable.

As well as involving people in the positive process of building up an idea, you should also ask others about what's wrong with your work, as suggested in IDEA 16, *Seek out criticism.*

Try another idea...

In terms of spitball, if you play with new people who you don't know very well, you have the added excitement of not knowing what they're going to throw back at you. You also don't really know how they're going to receive your idea, so even as you're speaking you may find yourself revising and adjusting what you're saying based on how your fellow spitballers are reacting – are they looking at you intently, fidgeting or staring out of the window?

It's no coincidence that another baseball term is used to describe those moments when your spitball has become a full-blow 'pitch'. Pitching is a key skill for people who want to make a living from their creativity. It involves a lot of repetition, both in terms of rehearsing your pitch and also ramming home to your audience the key attractions of your proposition. It is also about targeting and having a good aim – you need to make sure that your pitch is relevant to your audience and 'hits the mark'. You also want to be clear that you don't want them tampering with your idea illegally, or – worse – running off with it; both potential problems for all serious ballplayers.

'Write your first draft with your heart. Rewrite with your head.'
From the film *Finding Forrester*

Defining idea...

How did it go?

Q   I got bored by the repetition. Do I have to keep going over the same old things *ad nauseam*?

A   *The most likely explanation for your getting bored is that the idea you kept repeating just didn't stand up to that level of scrutiny – perhaps it was just a boring idea. Perhaps, too, you were repeating the same thing over and over again without any sense of change or development. The whole point of the process is to keep re-presenting and recasting your ideas in a new light each time – not the same old light. So always think about how you're going to jazz things up each time – for yourself as much as for anyone else. Even if this occasionally leads you down false paths, the journey will be worth it.*

Q   I get really nervous about pitching in front of people. Is there something else I can do?

A   *Don't give up. If you keep doing it, you'll eventually overcome your nerves and gain more confidence. That's another reason to repeat, repeat, repeat. It calms you down.*

41

Lie, flim-flam, embellish, elaborate

Using nonsense language and telling tall tales can test your ideas to the limit. It can also show up their strengths and weaknesses.

Creative people love embellishment. Other people might like to call this 'not quite telling the truth', but we don't usually worry about such minor details.

A little bit of exaggeration can make a run-of-the mill story into something special and entertaining. In the same way, if you stretch the credibility of your ideas, you actually might find you add more life to them. On the other hand, you may stretch them to breaking point – but at least you will have found out where that breaking point is.

We are big fans of nonsense. It made no sense at first, for example, for the central protagonist of our online Greek island entertainment 'Mount Kristos' to be an

Here's an idea for you... **Try taking something you're spinning out – a proposal, a first draft or presentation – and give it the nonsense treatment. You may be surprised by how much it freshens your perception of what you're really doing.**

obsessive Jim Morrison fan (except that Tim thought it would be funny and it reminded him of his sister's music collection). But in the end, this totally irrational decision brought with it a whole load of great ideas about musical performance, rock gods, identification, premature death and dressing up in funny ways that all really helped to unravel what the project was about, giving the piece its final shape and peculiar logic.

Quite often one only has to exaggerate one aspect of a very straight and sensible work in order to create a massive effect. In the world of caricature and cartoons, for example, it's not unusual for artists to pick out just one facial characteristic of a famous person in order to nail them in the eyes of the public. Think of Steve Bell's depiction of Tony Blair with his one mad staring eye, or Gerald Scarfe's stretching of Richard Nixon's nose.

Exaggeration can apply to all forms of creativity. By making things bigger (or smaller) than they actually are, you change their point of reference. Think of all those 1950s 'horror' movies that feature giant spiders or giant ants. Or *The Fantastic Voyage*, in which a very tiny Raquel Welch travels around inside a man's body (it's not as good as we've made it sound…).

Defining idea... **'Curiouser and curiouser!'**
LEWIS CARROLL, *Alice in Wonderland*

There, in fact, is the whole point of embellishment and exaggeration: you want your ideas to be better than they sounded at first. You want everything to be taller and brighter and wide and sleeker. You want the creative fish you've landed to be a whopper.

Building up things to look bigger and better than they're supposed to be – or indeed are – can get people's backs up. So can IDEA 12, *Take risks.*

Try another idea...

You probably also want to define the limits of your project or idea, and by rambling on and adding new (imaginary) features you'll very quickly get to the point where you know you're being silly and have to stop.

So do stretch credibility. Tell people that you're going to crucify yourself as soon as you've worked out how to bang the last nail in. Ramble on to the point of absurdity about how you're going to get Harrison Ford to wear a false moustache and meet you in a hotel in the Rockies. People will be entertained by this, we promise you. People will laugh (maybe at you rather than with you, but they'll laugh). And maybe, just maybe, amidst all the bullshit and lies, you may discover your next good idea...

'The trouble about man is twofold. He cannot learn truths which are too complicated; he forgets truths which are too simple.'
REBECCA WEST

Defining idea...

185

The other way to extend and stretch your work in silly ways is to actively allow it to fall into the realms of nonsense. The master of this is Lewis Carroll, author of *Alice in Wonderland* and also the man who gave us (in *Jabberwocky*):

'Twas brillig, and the slithy toves
Did gyre and gimble in the wabe.
All mimsy were the borogoves,
And the mome raths outgrabe.'

Sure it's nonsense, but somehow we still know what he means. The other master of the art of nonsense language was Professor Stanley Unwin. Not only did he write nonsense language, he used it in his everyday life: 'Professor Unlow recitely kindly. Delivering joyfull roundness on all-gathering (sitting quietly-softly), hanging-roundlow. Deep joy. Goodly byelode.'

Defining idea...

'**Man has always sacrificed truth to his vanity, comfort and advantage. He lives...by make-believe.**'
W. SOMERSET MAUGHAM

Q   **I hate lying in all its forms – even lying on my bed gives me backache. Can't I just let my work stand on its merits?**

A   *We're not asking you to lie as such, but rather enjoy the construction of a harmless tall tale that you might hear in your local pub of an evening (so it'll be about ferret rustling, no doubt). If your creative activity centres around documentary or history, then certainly you have a duty ultimately to stick to the facts, but even in these cases you may want to use exaggeration at certain points explicitly to make a point.*

Q   **I think I over-embellished. Do you?**

A   *It is tempting to keeping adding layer upon layer to your work because you're so excited about the possibilities. But by doing this you can end up with something rather baroque. In some periods of your life you'll probably like the idea of this kind of layering and complexity. At other times you'll yearn for simplicity. The good news about engaging in over-embellishment is that you'll teach yourself when to stop.*

How did it go?

187

42

Be in the picture

So you've gone on holiday, taken some snaps, got them developed, put them in an album and shelved it. There's surely more to it than that...isn't there?

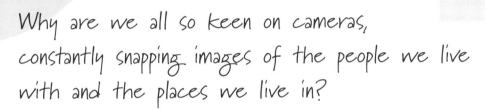

Why are we all so keen on cameras, constantly snapping images of the people we live with and the places we live in?

It has been said many times before that we photograph to remember, and to a large extent it is the fear that we might forget something about a particular experience that drives us on.

Holidays are a particular time when we can feel naked without a camera. It's funny, then, how unimaginative we can be about the photos we take on holiday. The key issue about holiday snaps, of course, is who takes them. If you're always the principal photographer, it means (rather sadly) that you're hardly ever in the shot. Quite a lot of dads become rather shadowy figures in photo albums as a result of this.

Here's an idea for you...

Digital photos are highly editable. Import them into a software application such as Adobe Photoshop and you can apply all manner of special effects. On a simpler level, crop your pics so that what was the centre of attention becomes peripheral. Often in taking a portrait you capture something unusual in the background that you didn't actually see at the time, which you can highlight. In essence, within every digital photo there are hundreds of 'versions' all waiting to be revealed by your creative eye.

One way of countering this is to get yourself in lots of other people's holiday photographs. (Must-read author Geoff Dyer has written a novel all about this called *The Search*, in which at one point a missing man's afternoon is reconstructed using hundreds of tourist photographs.) If you're feeling cheeky enough, don't even ask to be in the picture, just barge on in. In this way, instead of only being in your own photo album, you'll have created your own distributed exhibition of images of yourself in collections all around the world. Alternatively, offer to take photos of other people on holiday – and then shoot pictures they weren't expecting (of yourself!).

One man we know of on the Web decided not to bother with photos of people at all. He simply takes pictures of every holiday meal he's ever been served and posts them on the internet.

To a large extent, photo albums are another form of the collecting and archiving urge we've talked about elsewhere. How many of us have a box somewhere stuffed with photos that we never look at? Or perhaps you're the opposite and spend hours organising your collection into a neat series of albums.

Defining idea...

'The world just does not fit conveniently into the format of a 35mm camera.'
W. EUGENE SMITH, photojournalist

With the advent of digital technology the problems of how to share your photos have largely been resolved. You can email them to anyone in the world just a few seconds after you've taken them. As an alternative, there are a number of online photo gallery sites that allow you to annotate and display your photos in dynamic ways for the whole world to see.

Train yourself to look for more unusual images by reading IDEA 11, *Look at things another way.*

Try another idea...

One leading-edge online service at the moment is Flickr at www.flickr.com, which not only gives you your own page to show off your photos in several different sizes (thumbnail, medium and large), but also allows other people (if they have access rights) to leave comments on each photo. A chat system is also in place so that you can talk in real time over the internet about an image that has only just been captured. You can upload photos from your digital camera easily, but if you prefer, you can email them to the system or send them directly from a cameraphone. You can also post any of your Flickr photos directly to your blog.

Before this starts to sound too much like an advert, it's as well to remember that there's very little point in going to all this effort to let people see your photos if they aren't actually any good. However, if you're going to go to all this effort to organise your collection, chances are you'll start getting a bit more picky about what you show. And there's no excuse – with a digital camera you don't need to get every photo you take 'developed', so you can dump the bad snaps without anyone ever knowing that you took them in the first place.

'There are always two people in every picture: the photographer and the viewer.'
ANSEL ADAMS

Defining idea...

191

Q **All my photos are really blurry and useless. The only experimentation they are suitable for is finding different ways to throw them in the bin. Should I just give up?**

A   Most new digital cameras have an automatic setting that compensates for your shortcomings as a photographer. Read the manual (radical, we know) and just check you have this set up properly. Blurry photos don't have to be useless, mind. They can make really good backgrounds for slides with text, or they can be the jumping-off point for thoughts about more abstract images in general. With the growth of camera phones, blurriness, in fact, is almost de rigueur in proving the 'nowness' of your snap.

Q **I like this idea of a 'distributed exhibition' of my images, but I'd like to be able to see the results myself, not have them languishing in someone else's collection. Any thoughts?**

A   Why not try getting your images into the growing number of community photo collections on the Web? The Mirror Project, 'a growing community of like-minded individuals who have photographed themselves in all manner of reflective surfaces', is a great place to start. It's at www.mirrorproject.com

43

Play creative Jenga

The British do this with celebrities all the time, but there's more to building things up and then knocking them down than just sadistic pleasure.

If you don't know what Jenga is, you should get down to your local toy shop and buy yourself a set soon.

It's a very simple game really. You start by building a tower with a set of plain wooden bricks. Players then take it in turns to remove the bricks one at a time – without causing the tower to fall.

We like this game not only because it's amazing how many different types of tower you can build using the same standard set of blocks, but also because it shows you that successful structures rely as much on what you're prepared to take away as on what you decide to leave in place. (Oh, and it's noisy.)

We once attended a talk by Jason Swinscoe of the Cinematic Orchestra where he described one of his methods of music composition. He'd start with a favourite sample or loop from one of his favourite movie composers (Bernard Herrman, for

Here's an idea for you...

Take a piece of work you're happy with and remove one thing from it. Now add something that is completely unrelated – and see if the resulting piece stands up or falls down. And if it does fall, does it do so quickly? Slowly? All in one go? Bit by bit? And what pattern does the broken item (or 'new work') make when everything is finally lying in pieces? Even in these moments of destruction you might find something interesting and beautiful.

example) and then he'd build up layers of sounds and beats, sequences and other loops around it. When he felt he had finished his creative input, he would do one final thing – remove the original loop, the source of inspiration for the whole piece, to see if what was left could survive on its own terms.

This sounded to us exactly like Jenga. And we realised that it's a method you can apply to many other areas of creativity. Take a look at some of your own creative work and see if you can isolate the basic building blocks, both in terms of perceivable elements or attributes (specific sections, words, colours, columns, etc.), and in terms of the ideas and concepts which helped the work come into being. By doing this, you should already be looking at your work in a different way – seeing it as a series of dependencies and interrelated pieces rather than as a whole.

Now having surveyed and catalogued those pieces, start taking some away. If we're looking at, say, a photograph, you could physically crop it so that we see only two-thirds of what the photographer saw. If it's a digital image, you could remove specific sets of pixels, or take away specific parts of the pictures – rub out the person whose portrait you were taking and leave an empty space instead. Does this photo perhaps stand up as some kind of 'still life'? Is the absence of the sitter actually informing the piece?

Naturally, as you take things away, there will be a point where what you have simply isn't enough any more and it collapses into a formless mess. But this is information in its own right. You now know so much more about how your work actually 'works'. And here's a question – if you repeat the process again but take the same parts out *in a different order*, does the piece still fall down at the same point?

Deliberately breaking things or pulling them apart needn't be seen as a purely destructive act, as IDEA 10, *Smash it up*, shows.

Try another idea…

Taking the analogy further, what about propping your tower up with something other than a brick? This is cheating when it comes to Jenga, but there's no such thing as cheating in personal creativity – just short cuts and new ways of looking at things.

Or why not play a different type of Jenga, where instead of just taking away bricks, you actually replace each one with something very non-brick-like? Not only would the resulting structure look very different each time – but the point at which the tower falls down would be that much more unpredictable.

'You must break through old structures, develop broader structures, break through those and develop still broader structures.'
RAM DASS

Defining idea…

195

How did
it go?

Q   **It's a nice concept, but I don't see how you can play Jenga with pieces of writing or a set of oil paintings. Can you enlighten me?**

A   *In both your examples, you need to list out what the building blocks of the work are. In the case of writing, these will be particular words, phrases – or even letters of the alphabet. In the case of oil painting, there are the colours used, the thickness of the paint, the type of brushstroke and so on. Now remove something. So in Wordsworth's famous line: 'I wandered lonely as a cloud', removing the 'a's would give 'I wndered lonely s cloud'. Remove the 'u's and you get: 'I wandered lonely as a clod'. Turning to painting, what would be the effect of removing clouds from some of Constable's paintings? Or cropping the painting to remove the whole sky? Following the Jenga substitution rule, if we replaced Wordsworth's textual cloud with Constable's painted cloud, we'd suddenly have a visual poem! Is that just silly? Or does it show more clearly the compositional elements and their interdependency?*

Q   **But that's not how you play Jenga. You don't simply remove blocks from the tower, you keep putting them back on top until the tower falls. Don't you?**

A   *OK, so we've taken liberties here to make a point. But just think about your idea as a structure. What happens if you take a key element from the foundation and add it to the edge? Make the main point of your argument a footnote. Make the full-page image around which you are basing your layout a thumbnail in the corner. Is there some other, better element that can take its place?*

44

Faking it

How to appropriate other people's talents without upsetting them. 'I'll copy yours if you copy mine...'

There is a long tradition in all areas of creative practice of learning through imitation. Well that's the polite way of putting it, anyway.

'Standing on the shoulders of giants' is an expression often used to describe the way an artist draws from the ideas of talented people who have gone before. And it's true that if you stand on other people's shoulders, your view of the world is generally improved.

Young writers often set themselves the task of writing in the style of a famous poet or novelist. It allows them to get 'under the bonnet' of an author, as it were, and work out the basic mechanics of how things work and how certain structures and effects can be achieved.

At art school, undergraduates are often asked to attempt a painting in the style of an old master. Again, it helps them get to grips with the specifics of technique –

Here's an idea for you...

By copying one another (or 'collaborating', to use a more modern word for it), a group of artists can help develop their own distinctive and unique elements within an agreed set of stylistic or technical rules. So if you can find a gang of creative people who all like working the same way, join in and use your imitation of others to expand your own palette. It's true that, after a while, gangs can get a bit *too* cliquey, but being like everyone else at an early point of your creative development is just fine.

brush selection, working with oils as opposed to acrylics, colour selection, composition. etc. (And it can help pay their fees.)

The old masters themselves ran studios with a number of apprentices whose job it was to paint like the great man himself (and alas, yes, they were all men); indeed, paintings ascribed to a single painter such as Titian or Raphael are often actually the work of several people all working under the direction of the named artist.

This practice still goes on today. Many of Damien Hirst's spot paintings, for example, were not painted by Hirst, but by assistants in his studio. Although it's yet to be proved whether any of these people will go on to become great artists in their own right, many of those who undertook apprenticeships with the Italian masters did make names for themselves and opened their own studios in turn. Imitation, in this case, was absolutely critical for the development not only of creative individuals, but also of schools of painting and artistic movements.

Belonging to a school of creative thought or a particular gang of artists can be incredibly exciting and productive. Joining a gang or school implies a certain number of shared values or rules, so you are immediately supplied with some kind of framework or support for your work.

It's also absolutely fine to copy your heroes. In fact, you may not even understand why this person is your hero until you attempt the imitation. As Bruce Mau points out in his *Incomplete Manifesto for Growth*: 'Imitate. Don't be shy about it. Try to get as close as you can. You'll never get all the way, and the separation might be truly remarkable.' By imitating someone in this way, you're not only paying homage to them, you're working out what it takes to create a work that you have instinctively recognised as great. And as Mau notes, there'll be something in the difference between your results and the original output that is recognisably yours – and could become the first sparks of a highly original work of your own.

Imagining yourself as another person is another form of imitation that can help you approach your concepts and problems in a different way. Find out more in IDEA 23, *Play your part*.

Try another idea...

Alluding to great works, or resetting them in a contemporary setting, is also a great way of changing your audience's perception of an object or an artefact. Many of Andy Warhol's greatest works, for example, are 'copies' of other people's photographs, but are still recognised as original works of art. His famous soup tins were in fact not 'made' by him at all, but were the creative work of the graphic designer who came up with the soup label. But by re-presenting the tins and changing the context in which we see them (the gallery rather than the supermarket), Warhol changed our perception of soup tins forever, and in the process very definitely established his own creative style.

'The secret to creativity is knowing how to hide your sources.'
ALBERT EINSTEIN

Defining idea...

How did it go? **Q** **Imitating great people's work just made me feel unoriginal and useless. How is this going to help my style – or my self-confidence?**

A *The exercise here is nothing to do with originality. Really, don't worry about that. And we're not expecting you to suddenly be able to draw like Picasso, write like Hemingway or give a speech like Churchill (after all, it took them years to achieve their mastery). Just have a go. The point here is to get to grips with someone else's technique, and through doing that you'll gain a better understanding of what your own skills and style might be. If they'd had a chance to copy you, who knows how much better they'd have become?*

Q **So what's the difference between imitation and just being derivative?**

A *When you're engaged in an act of imitation you shouldn't be trying to put too much of yourself into the work. You are basically trying to perform like someone else. A derivative work is when you try to express yourself in your own way – only to find that you haven't yet developed your own way! Repeating someone else's tricks can be a good thing. But if you don't add a little bit of your own magic, your creative work is always going to live in the shadow of someone else's.*

45

Give it all away

Do all that hard work and then give it away for nothing? Madness lies that way, surely? Don't be so certain.

Suspicious about giving your ideas away for nothing? That's understandable. Indeed, unless you're working in a hermetically sealed vacuum, you've probably tried your damnedest to stop others from stealing them already.

But if you're not prepared to share your knowledge and experience with others, you're probably going to take twice as long to get anything done. You're also going to foster a culture of covetousness and non-giving in others that runs directly counter to the spirit of creative expression.

People are actually pretty generous when it comes to giving. Did you know, for example, that in Britain people spend on average 4% of their annual income on Christmas presents? So says Roger Highfield in his book *The Science of Christmas*. He also points out that roughly 8% of the national economy is devoted to producing articles that will end up being given away as presents. That's a hell of a lot of creative energy to expend on freebies!

Here's an idea for you...

The whole act of 'giving' is shrouded in ritual. We wrap and decorate our gifts, attach cards and labels, create elaborate ceremonies and specific places in which to leave them, whether it's under a Christmas tree or on a pillow. Consider these peripheral elements of your work: the packaging, the labelling, the means of distribution and delivery. Does the way in which you 'wrap' your idea change the way it is received?

Sharing and gift-giving are actually great ways of distributing your creative ideas in a practical way. First and foremost they gain you value in terms of esteem and use – and later (sometimes) you can convert that value into hard cash.

Back in primitive times, man understood the practical value of sharing. A hunter would kill an antelope and hand out meat to the whole tribe. Maybe there weren't quite equal shares (your kids would be higher up the order than the one-legged doom-merchant in the corner), but for the hunter it made sense to be seen by everyone in the tribe as fair and generous, as well as capable of accomplishing something as difficult and highly skilled as catching an antelope. This put him in a very powerful social position. Besides, eating a whole antelope is a pretty big task and beyond even the most ravenous of hunters, so sharing didn't actually cost him anything in lost food.

In other cultures, more sophisticated acts of giving and trading have emerged over time. In Papua New Guinea, there is *Kula*, whereby each person wears an armband and a necklace made from shell. The idea is that as you travel around the towns and islands carrying out your trade, you exchange these bits of costume jewellery with your trading partners

Defining idea...

'Give to get.'
Sir GERALD INOMYNTE, President and CEO, XPT plc

– an armband for a necklace, a necklace for an armband. No trade of other goods can take place without this exchange. A circle of good trading relationships is thus secured by this circulation of jewellery, which also acts as a visible sign of who you know and where you've been.

If you feel you have something to give, we can help you find more people to give it to. Go to IDEA 34, *Network near, network far.*

Try another idea...

Another famous example is *potlatch*. This North American Indian ritual involved the lavish reciprocal distribution of gifts, and developed a competitive edge: could you give away more and lovelier stuff something than the thing you received? Once the hard cash of the Europeans came into play, *potlatch* somewhat lost the plot, with people not just giving away vast amounts of wealth but actually publicly destroying possessions just to show how easily they could do without them. In some parts of the country, the ritual was actually banned.

All these models should be considered when preparing to share your creativity. And before you say that this kind of stuff is just ancient ceremonial nonsense, bear in mind that many of the world's great scientists operate within gift economies. The scientists with the highest status are not those who possess the most knowledge, but those who have contributed the most to their field – by publishing more.

'To make a gift of something to someone is to make a present of some part of oneself.'
MARCEL MAUSS, ethnographer

Defining idea...

On the internet, too, a lot of sharing goes on without money or politics getting in the way. Quite often people barter skill for skill: 'You code my Web page and I'll give you a cool animation to put on your site', etc. Or people simply put the fruits of their programming labour up for all to download as shareware.

How did
it go?

Q **I'm into sharing, but I also want to protect my copyright. How do I do both?**

A *Copyright protection can sometimes be seen as the enemy of these emerging modern gift economies, but it needn't be the case. A relatively new organisation called Creative Commons is pioneering new forms of 'reasonable, flexible copyright in the face of increasingly restrictive default rules'. This involves easy access to standard proforma copyright statements over the internet, whereby you get to say clearly how you're prepared to share your material. For more information on this go to http://creativecommons.org.*

Q **If no one actually buys my stuff, how can I tell if it's any good?**

A *Put that another way – if you put a price on your output but don't sell anything anyway, what does that actually tell you? That you're charging too much? That your product was poorly marketed or distributed badly? That it was the wrong time of day/year to be trying to charge for that stuff? Or that your stuff really is crap? It actually tells you all and none of the above. You really need to have many more criteria for valuing your work than just the cover price, so feedback from people receiving freebies can be hugely important.*

46

Tools of the trade – technology

Hi tech – when to use it, when to lose it. Be more a surfer than a serf.

OK, so we admit it, we make our living out of mucking around with technology, so we're pretty much in love with the stuff.

On the other hand, we completely acknowledge that there's a time and place for geekery, and if technology is taking you away from experiencing real life to the full (or 'farting about', as Kurt Vonnegut likes called it), then it may well be getting in the way of your creative development and maybe you should just say no.

We would rather say 'maybe', because good technology should actually enhance your daily life. In fact, it may even change your daily life (more on this in a mo'). Really, the only kind of technology you need to be sceptical about is bad technology. Sadly, there's a lot of it about. Most people's experience of personal computers, for example, is that they are for the most part overly complex, unreliable clunky machines that never print properly when you most want them to and 'hang' when you're in a hurry. Only by getting interested in how or why they go wrong do most people master ways of being creative or productive with a computer.

Here's an idea for you... **Test any new technology you're thinking of using with Marshall McLuhan's questions: (1) 'What does the new medium or technology extend?' For a bicycle, this would be the foot; for a phone, the voice. (2) 'What does it make obsolete?' (3) 'What is retrieved?' (4) 'What does the technology reverse into if it is overextended?'**

So it's good to be sceptical. Good questions to always ask yourself about any new way of doing things include:

■ What does this enable me to do that I'm not already doing?

■ What does this enable me to leave behind that was frustrating me or holding me back?

■ What new acts of synthesis can I achieve with this?

■ What have I got to lose by adopting this new approach?

Defining idea... *'Technology is another word for tool. There was a time when nails were high-tech.'*
TOM CLANCY

If the answers to all these questions are positive, then embrace the new way with open arms and mind. If not, then wait for the next new thing – it won't be long in coming.

The wired world's favourite guru, Marshall McLuhan, has a rather neat way of describing any new media (aka new technology in this context) as 'extensions of man', by which he means (we think) extensions of both our senses and our abilities. 'We shape our tools and afterwards our tools shape us,' he says. In a more high-falutin' passage he describes how our whole society can be shaped by technology:

If you still need convincing that technology could help you be more creative, read what we've got to say about mobile devices in IDEA 26, *Boys' toys and girls' gadgets.*

Try another idea...

'Persons grouped around a fire or candle for warmth or light are less able to pursue independent thoughts, or even tasks, than people supplied with electric light. In the same way, the social and educational patterns latent in automation are those of self-employment and artistic autonomy.'

For creative people like you, the idea that technology can be used as some kind of divining rod to discover how society and the world might be changing is reason enough to get stuck in, we say.

Add to that the idea that artists might actually have some kind of influence over the ways things change by being tech-savvy and we can see no reason why you wouldn't make the move from the ivory tower to the control tower.

'Do you realize if it weren't for Edison we'd be watching TV by candlelight?'
AL BOLISKA, 1960s radio personality

Defining idea...

How did it go?

Q **I hate computers. They don't do anything that I would consider useful or interesting. Why should I bother with them?**

A *A lot of people suffer from technophobia. And we're all fed a lot of negative images about computers through the media. For example, when was the last time you saw computers used for good in a movie? Usually techy people are either eccentric geeks or evil masterminds who want to rule the world. You really need to fight this kind of prejudice and be a bit more open minded about what computers could do for you. (By the way, for a funny list of 'bad technology' used by sci-fi writers check out www.wirewd.com/cybrpunk/cpbtech.html)*

Q **I feel like I need some kind of formal training in order to get to grips with technology. What do you suggest?**

A *That's not a bad idea. Most people don't ever read the manuals that come with a computer and simply bluff their way through. But there comes a time when your productivity could be dramatically improved by learning how a computer really works and maybe getting some lessons about a particular piece of software. Check out your local advice bureau or skills centre and you'll probably find courses available at pretty good prices.*

Q **I don't like being dependent on technology for anything. Don't I have a choice?**

A *Look around you. Technology is everywhere. You are already dependent upon it. And things are only likely to get worse (or better, to our way of thinking). Could you seriously do without everything electrical in your life, for example?*

47

Get Googling

Googling is like mud-wrestling for the mind. You can wade in and get good and filthy mucking about with search engines and other services, and it's more fun than it first appears.

If you don't have internet access in your home yet, we suggest that you consider getting it.

We appreciate that investing in a computer with the appropriate software and then paying out a monthly subscription can be quite an ask. But we guarantee that you will find so much creative stimulation online that it'll all be worth it.

Your first stop on the Web – once you've abandoned your access provider's invariably cluttered and useless portal – will almost certainly be a search engine that will help you find your way around the squillions of sites there are to see. And the most popular search engine of the moment is Google.

If nothing else, Google is an absolutely fantastic tool for brainstorming ideas. Feed it with more or less any term you like and it'll bring you a host of sites to look at within milliseconds. Many of them will be useless to you. But we guarantee that

Here's an idea for you...

If you want to know who Tim Wright might actually be, you can also go to Googlism (www.googlism.com). Type in his name and this is a tiny extract of what you'll get: tim wright is currently sailing from gibraltar to the caribbean; tim wright is a glowing exception; tim wright is not far behind; tim wright is an asset to your company; tim wright is renowned for his bold maritime paintings. The curious thing is that none of these Tim Wrights is yours truly. Type your own name into Googlism and see what all your name-sakes are up to. Maybe there are things in the list that will inspire you, or lead you into some new area of creative activity. Tim, for example, would like to be the Tim Wright who performs as the magician Skildini and is in training as we speak.

you'll find something quite unexpected that sparks your imagination. Without Google, for example, Tim would never know so much about the bauxite mining industry that now acts as a backdrop to one of his projects. And Rob would be without his vast collection of cheese-related artwork.

Google isn't just about websites, though. Search under *Images* and suddenly you're confronted by an amazing library of photos and digital artwork to play with. With image searching you often have to be persistent and click through a number of pages to find the good stuff – but there is no better instant text-to-image conversion system that we know of.

To add even more chance to your creative research, instead of hitting the 'Search' button after entering your search term, you can always hit 'I'm Feeling Lucky' and be taken automatically to the first site on the search list. This can again provide you with yet more surprises and stimulation. (For example, type in 'French military victories' and hit 'I'm Feeling Lucky' and see what you turn up.)

A number of people have dreamed up other strange uses for Google that are fun to try. The most popular of them all is googlewhacking (www.googlewhack.com/), whereby you have to look for combinations of common words which only appear within the same page once on the whole of the Web (as indexed by Google). Recent examples include: twinkly fatherliness, ballsiest despot and dyslexic sharksucker.

Googlealerts (www.googlealert.com) is a neat way to do your searching in the background, rather than as your main activity. This service will even send you email alerts about new search items.

Another silly Google service is googlefight (www.googlefight.com), a site that allows you to put key words up against each other and find out which ones yield more search results. The result of the authors' googlefight, for example, was a drubbing for Rob: Tim Wright (1,260,000 results) versus Rob Bevan (79,500 results).

If you like being creative with Web tools, you should also experiment a little with your email. For suggestions, go to IDEA 34, *Network near, network far.*

Try another idea...

'eBay is becoming the most important way for people to exchange goods. Exchanging goods, exchanging information, and exchanging culture are the three most important activities undertaken by human beings, with the exception of exchanging fluids.'
CORY DOCTOROW, author and Outreach Coordinator for the Electronic Frontier Foundation

Defining idea...

211

How did it go?

Q **My search term brought up so many sites I didn't know where to start. If I'd visited each and every one of them rather than turning my computer off and going down the pub, I'd still be trawling now. Will it always be like this?**

A *You can always narrow down the field by adding more words to your search or looking for a specific term, which you do by typing it in with quote marks around it. Google isn't ever going to do all the work for you. You may well need to go through several pages of search returns to find things that excite your interest, but it's still quicker and easier then most other forms of creative research.*

Q **I think the searches are fiddled sometimes so that the same sites come to the top of the list every time. Have you noticed that?**

A *Well spotted! Google is a business and it does take money from people who want to have their site associated strongly with specific search terms. It is also true that Google stores and analyses the searches people make, so if you're of a paranoid disposition, you should probably not google for too much seditious or illegal material. If you want to know about Google's not always clear-cut business practices, keep in touch with www.google-watch.org*

212

Become an alpha geek

Why you should learn to program and get creative with computing – even if the result is a right Jackson Pollock of a program.

Recently the term 'geek' has been used not only to describe those nerdy tech support blokes you find in every office, but also as a label for anyone doing really interesting things with technology.

Tim O'Reilly is a seasoned geek spotter. In fact, he makes a living out of organising conferences and writing books on the subject. This is what he had to say at the O'Reilly Emerging Technology Conference about a particular form of geek – the hacker:

'And so, there is a fundamental principle underlying a lot of what we do, and that is that hackers – and I think of hackers not as people who break into systems, but hackers as people like most of you who are very comfortable with technology – who

Here's an idea for you...

If programming isn't for you, have a go at some serious cookery. A lot of programmers are also keen cooks, and it's not for nothing that programs are often known as 'recipes', software manuals 'cookbooks' and coding workshops 'kitchens'. Cooking is another highly technical activity that's more art than science, and that might help you think about your creative work in new ways.

get a new toy, who get a new piece of code, who get a new service and you say, "Wow, they didn't do it quite right. I know what I can do; I can make it better. I can use it in some way that they didn't quite expect."'

This is the principle: be comfortable with technology and make it do what YOU want it to do. It's a bit like learning to cook: the more you are able to do yourself, the less you have to put up with what's put on a plate in front of you – and the more you can appreciate the artistry of others.

Even a passing familiarity with how software works can help you understand more about the technology around you. And since there's getting to be more and more of it around you virtually every day, it makes a lot of sense to feel a bit more in control of it and by extension your environment.

Think of how old and crusty people sound when they tell you they don't even know how to set the VCR. How lazy and pathetic is that?! Well, that's how old and crusty you're going to look in a couple of decades' time if you can't get to grips with even the most basic computer setup.

Programming can actually be a real salvation for creative people who aren't that good at linearity (like Rob). By which we mean, if you can't really get your head around something like writing out a piece of prose in the conventional order of beginning, middle and end, then maybe programming is for you. By getting to grips with code, you can create great non-linear structures where everyone starts in different beginnings, meets different people at different points in the middle – and there is no end.

> If we haven't quite persuaded you to give programming a go, don't worry. There are other ways of supplementing your lack of a particular skill, as covered in IDEA 35, *Know what you can't do.*

Try another idea...

Programming needn't be that complicated or intimidating either. For example, you might have heard of the term 'object orientated programming' (OOP), the current 'latest and greatest' programming method. Sounds techy already, right? But an 'object' is really only a software bundle of related variables (ingredients) and methods (processes: cooking, stirring, boiling, baking). You use the software objects to model real-world objects you find in everyday life, just as you might combine ingredients (and their tastes, smells and flavours) using various cooking techniques to make a first-rate dinner.

Now that doesn't sound so hard, does it?

> '*Man is driven to create; I know I really love to create things. And while I'm not good at painting, drawing, or music, I can write software.*' YUKIHIRO MATSUMOTO, creator of Ruby

Defining idea...

How did
it go?

Q **Programming has always struck me as a nerdy, solitary kind of activity that involves lots of maths. It is, isn't it?**

A *No, it isn't. It's more like poetry, using precise syntactic rules and a whole wealth of vocabulary to express yourself and your ideas. Yes, it can be solitary, but a lot of new 'agile' programming methodologies, such as Extreme Programming (XP) (see www.extremeprogramming.org), place the emphasis on collaboration. The customer (i.e. the user) and the XP programmer work through the same computer (which sounds pretty silly, but apparently delivers better results in terms of programming quality than two people working at separate machines) to develop the program together. This early customer input means that the system built is actually designed to do the job it is intended for, rather than something that a few programmers thought it would be neat to build. So you see, programming can be pretty sensible and non-nerdy – and social too!*

Q **I wanted to give this a go, but there are so many computer languages – C, C++, Java, Perl, Python, SmallTalk, etc. Which should I choose?**

A *Try Ruby. Big in Japan and getting bigger in the west, it was invented in 1995 by Yukihiro Matsumoto (aka Matz). It's very simple, very powerful and has a small but growing community. Start by being ahead of the curve! Why Ruby? Well, the learning curve is low, and once you get over the first hump, you start to 'guess' how things work...and your guesses are often correct. Programming Ruby, by David Thomas and Andrew Hunt, is available free online (at www.rubycentral.com/book/index.html), and there's also a good online Ruby tutorial for the 'future programmer' (at http://pine.fm/LearnToProgram).*

49

Come back in the morning

Know when to put things on the back-burner, and how to let them simmer there rather than just grow cold or go mouldy.

You might very well claim to be a night-time person — an owl rather than a lark — but the fact is everyone works more effectively after a good night's sleep.

Fair enough, if it's getting late but you're motoring and 'in the zone', then stay up and feed off that feeling. Fair enough too if you have a deadline and simply must produce *something* for the next day. At some point, you may have to think tactically about what you can get away with, and burn a bit of night-oil thinking up good reasons why you're not going to deliver under the original terms of engagement. But never, ever bother bashing away at a problem late at night just for the sake of it, when you know in your heart of hearts you're not really solving anything. That really is a waste of time. And nobody will be impressed with your tired haggard expression unless the work itself has clearly been worth the effort.

If you have an imminent deadline, take your half-finished work to the meeting, admit your problems and ask for help in fixing them. Sometimes this makes everybody feel creative and valued. (Be careful how often you try and get away with this, by the way.) If your deadline is not so urgent, best leave it for several mornings (or months)!

In most cases, admitting defeat and coming back to something in the morning can really help not only to finally complete a piece of work in a good way – but also can ensure that you're in some kind of condition to really deliver at the critical moments.

According to Woody Allen, 'Eighty percent of success is showing up'. If you expend all your energy working fruitlessly through the night, you really aren't going to stand much chance of 'showing up' in the morning – either you'll be in bed fast asleep or you'll turn up at the office with your brain about as functional as a boiled pomegranate.

It really is true that you can see things differently in the morning light, especially if you're well rested and alert. Indeed, changes in light generally can throw a very different slant on your work. If you don't believe us, try working in different types of light, both artificial and natural. Experiment with a range of different light bulbs, perhaps. At different times of the day move to different rooms that have more or fewer windows, or face in a particular direction. Get up really early and sample the light at dawn (but don't stay up to do the same thing). Similarly, try working at dusk. (More accidents at work happen then than at any other time, by the way. You've been warned, so don't blame us.)

Defining idea... **'Why is it I get my best ideas in the morning while I'm shaving?'**
ALBERT EINSTEIN

Sleep can also bring with it all kinds of strange dreams and thoughts that may come to your aid in the morning. It's amazing, too, how just by letting time pass a problem can go away (shame it doesn't work with toothache). For most creative people it's tempting to think that things only happen because of your presence and your input. But actually things happen without you too. Plants still grow, the world still spins and often what seemed so awful yesterday isn't so bad today. Crucially, you may also find that if you leave something in this way, somebody else will come along with the necessary input to fix things.

Try another idea...

If you've bought into this idea, try to extract more creative capital from snoozing and dreaming after you read **IDEA 50, *Sleep on it.***

Defining idea...

'One must also accept that one has uncreative moments. The more honestly one can accept that, the quicker these moments will pass. One must have the courage to call a halt, to feel empty and discouraged.'
ETTY HILLESUM

How did it go?

Q I hate giving up on anything – even if it's past my bedtime. Wouldn't I be better off finishing it in one go?

A   *Abandoning something that isn't working right now can be emotionally difficult if you haven't got something else to move on to. You may well feel that you've failed yourself, or that you 'aren't really creative', or that all this was a bad idea from the start – but don't. Walking away from something actually gives it the chance to find its own way back to you. Maybe its current form isn't the right one for now. Maybe it's currently a painting, but will come back as a performance piece next year. Always store what you've got – never trash it – and bring it out for inspection at some later date. Bring it out, in fact, when you're stuck on something else and are having that same crisis all over again. If you do this with enough ideas and projects, you'll actually always have something to move on to – and that way you'll never actually be giving up on anything.*

Q I find it hard to stop. There's always something left to do. Where should I draw the line (and should I touch it up, once I've drawn it)?

A   *There's a sense in which no project is ever really finished, just abandoned. If you're the kind of person who goes on working on something long after everyone else would have abandoned it, maybe it's time to impose an overtime ban. Force yourself to go home early, arrange to meet friends when you would normally be working – or just take a holiday. Consider the words of W. Somerset Maugham: 'Perfection has one grave defect: it is apt to be dull.'*

50

Sleep on it

**There's more to being creative than simply creating things.
Learn how dreaming and being unconscious can help, too.**

*Quite a lot of famous creative people
keep a pen and notepad by the bed, so
that they can quickly capture any amazing
thoughts that occur to them in their sleep.*

Certainly the subconscious mind is a powerful tool – and your brain very definitely
keeps working even when you're asleep.

Some experts even see sleeping as a chance for your brain to let off some
metaphorical steam and finally link and categorise (i.e. make sense of) the vast
amount of sensory information it has been bombarded with during waking hours. A
really obvious example of how this works is the way actors and other public
performers who have the heavy task of memorising lots of speeches and texts find it
helpful to go through their work just before bedtime. By going to sleep with a basic
memorisation task on your mind, you can find that in the morning the brain has
done the job for you overnight.

Here's an idea for you...

If you don't believe us about memorisation, try doing this with a short poem. Read it through several times at bedtime, attempt to recite it without looking a couple of times, check where you went wrong and then sleep on it. In the morning, with just one quick read-through, try and recite the whole thing again over your cornflakes. Chances are you'll be nigh-on perfect. Within weeks, you too could become a walking fount of poetry. (You may find yourself breakfasting alone, though...)

Recording dreams is also a popular creative pastime, although opinion is pretty much split about what dreams can really tell us about ourselves. Inasmuch as it's a good discipline to document your inner life and to not let things slip away from you (as dreams so quickly do), we'd encourage you to write down your dreams. Just don't read too much into them. Tim, for example, often dreams of being on a bus trying to sing out loud the words to 'Mack The Knife' – even though he doesn't really know them – in an effort to 'summon' Rob. One could say this exemplifies something about how close Tim and Rob are creatively. On the other hand, it could mean Tim is simply harbouring thoughts of cutting Rob into little bits...

Einstein, one of the greatest creative thinkers of all time, was very taken with the power of dreams to aid our thinking. He often felt his best ideas came to him not necessarily when he was fully sleep, but when he was snoozing or half-awake. He called these 'periods of deep thought', and famously during one of these periods (after lunch, presumably) he imagined himself taking a train ride across space on a beam of light and from this experience developed the Theory of Relativity.

Other examples of this dream thinking, often used to solve seriously hard science problems, include Kekulé's doze about a circle of tail-to-mouth snakes in his fireplace that taught him the structure of the benzene ring, the basis of much organic chemistry. Or consider Elias Howe's nightmare of cannibals attacking him with spears that had holes in their blades. It was this experience that led to him inventing the sewing machine.

If you like the idea of doing things without too much conscious thought, maybe you should embrace the *dérive* mentioned in IDEA 28, *Drift*.

Try another idea...

Quite often, dreams offer us ways to visualise concepts and anxieties that we'd otherwise find it hard to articulate. We often talk about the symbolism of dreams – the big white horse, the locked door, flying and falling, going back to school, being naked in public – and there are mighty tomes written on this subject. (Start with Jung if you like, and keep going from there.)

But one of the great things about dreams is that they don't in fact make sense, and you often don't understand why your subconscious has been excited by particular images and sequences. Solving the puzzles offered by the subconscious mind has for centuries been a great starting point for artists and offers you a great tradition to draw from. Go to a big art gallery, for example, and check out all the paintings that either depict people sleeping or are based on a dream in some way. You're bound to find several. Similarly, pick out all the poems in a big anthology that are about dreaming and sleeping in some way. There'll be dozens.

'Dream lofty dreams, and as you dream, so shall you become. Your vision is the promise of what you shall at last unveil.'
JOHN RUSKIN

Defining idea...

In short, the good news is that it's not only OK to snooze, it's actually a positive thing to do. Just make sure you keep that notebook handy for when you wake up – and don't just dream about taking notes.

How did it go?

Q **I'm not a great one for writing down anything – let alone my dreams. Can't I just try to remember them instead?**

A *Whether you buy into this stuff or not, recording your dreams can be a useful exercise. Instead of writing down your dreams as text, why not try for a while to draw them out as a sequence of pictures? By treating your dreams in this way – like a movie rather than a book – you may well find interesting mappings and correlations with the creative work that you are engaged with. You may notice some things that perhaps you wouldn't have spotted were you referencing your dream as something written, or as something you've already subconsciously organised into a sensible 'narrative'.*

Q **I've tried priming my mind with ideas before going to bed but I spend hours tossing and turning, then wake up stressing about unfinished work. Are you sure this is a good idea?**

A *Maybe you're focusing on the problems rather than their possible solutions. Try not to prime yourself by thinking about what you have to do, instead try to work on a 'dummy' or a 'rough' idea and see if you dwell on that rather than the final finished article.*

51

Distraction loops

Sometimes worrying endlessly at a problem ties you in knots. But don't worry. There are things you can do to take your mind off a problem without completely giving up on it.

Ring-fencing long stretches of uninterrupted time that you can dedicate exclusively to your creative work can be hard work. Often there are interruptions — which are not always a bad thing.

You often need to 'sharpen pencils' and build up a head of steam before you really get going on something. Sometimes, when you're right in the middle of a piece of work, getting up and doing something else can be just what the creative doctor ordered. Some might say this is exactly what the coffee break was invented for – as a means of getting way from the coalface, engaging in the making and consuming of something simple for a short while, often in a relaxed social environment, with the added bonus of a jolt of caffeine (if you like your coffee caffeinated, that is).

Here's an
idea for
you...

Breathing exercises are themselves a form of distraction loop. Breathe in through your nose as you slowly count to four. Hold your breath for a count of two and then exhale through your mouth for a slow count of six. Repeat this at least a couple of dozen times and you'll find that by regulating your breathing, you will also have slowed down your heart beat and relaxed physically.

We call these little breaks 'distraction loops' because they are very often repetitive rituals whereby things happen the same way pretty much every time. Making a cup of coffee is a classic example of this: not only do you make your coffee in pretty much the same way every time, you often do it at the same time every day, too. It's also a circular or 'looping' exercise because you end up pretty much where you started – the cup is empty and you're back at work.

Looping is a musician's term for picking out a sequence of music or notes played by one instrument and repeating it over and over again to produce a core rhythmic track which you can then embellish, orchestrate and use to grow your own original compositions around.

If you want to understand the physical sensation of looping, think back to when you were a child and how you enjoyed swinging things on the end of a string – like a conker or yo-yo – or rotating circular objects – like a hula-hoop or a wheel. You would always find yourself doing it faster and faster until gravity and momentum were doing most of the work for you, and all you had to do to keep it going with minimal effort was flex your muscles or dip your arms

Defining
idea...

'Every exit is an entry somewhere else.'
TOM STOPPARD

or hands precisely in time with the rhythm. This is looping at its finest. Often, while maintaining the rhythm, your mind woud be freed to think of more ambitious ways of doing it – and you'd then try more advanced physical tricks or attempt to add more intricate looping sequences.

In effect, even as a child with a yo-yo or a hula-hoop, you were doing what a grown-up musician does with musical loops.

Small and simple repetitive tasks are also a way of calming the mind and the body. Sometimes creativity can be very stressful. You're in the middle of an idea and you're stuck. The clock is ticking. You have a deadline. You feel like you're banging you're head against a brick wall. You daren't take a break because you have so much to do – but you're not actually achieving anything by sticking at it either. Not only do you definitely need a break, but engaging in a distraction loop may also very well help you to calm down and return to the fray in a better state.

Build a physical loop into your working day. Mowing the lawn – if you have one – is a great distraction loop precisely because it involves going backwards and forwards over a piece of ground at a slow but steady pace. Swimming backwards and forwards in a pool is good for both unwinding and buying yourself some free thinking time. Both of these activities are very public and deliberately take you away from the coalface. But don't worry – you may well be about to uncover a rich new seam of creative endeavour.

...and another

Sometimes through repetition your distraction loops can become creative projects in their own right. Investigate further in IDEA 40, *Spit it out*.

Try another idea...

How did
it go?

Q **This all sounds like an excuse for running away when things get tough. Are you sure that's the way to succeed?**

A   *Sometimes a distraction loop is indeed what you might call a 'tactical retreat' – and it's none the worse for that. Sometimes the best response to a tough or dangerous situation is to stand back, remove yourself and let time pass. You might even want to think about gathering reinforcements: you could use your coffee break to ask someone for a bit of help with what you're trying to do. Now that's not cowardice at all – it's actually quite smart.*

Q **How can I tell the difference between a distraction and a pointless chore?**

A   *No chore is pointless. You can find interest in everything that you do if you're a truly creative person. That isn't some tired old line, either. It's a challenge!*

Q **My distraction loop has become so engaging that my main work is really suffering. In fact, it's turning into a bit of a distraction! How can I stop it?**

A   *The short answer is don't – yet. That's often how new creative projects gain momentum. They start as a little distraction and then become the main event. Go with the flow and see where it leads. Perhaps your main work will be improved in the meantime by your taking a back seat for a while.*

Do absolutely nothing

Learn to just be.

After all this creativity, you probably need a rest.

It can actually be quite hard to do absolutely nothing. For a start, you have an inquisitive, creative mind that finds interest in everything around you (if you don't, then this book has failed in its mission). Even when you're just sitting in your back garden, or slobbing out on the couch, your brain is at work, taking in new stimuli and synthesising ideas. You are never at rest, even if other people think you are.

Sadly, creative people can do a very good impression of being useless layabouts. Because of this, other people can be a real problem when you're trying to get away from it all. As soon as you look like you're doing nothing, they will often step in and try to 'keep you busy'.

In these modern times, a lot of us work from home or exist in weird hybrid spaces between work and play – and we're none the worse for that. Trouble is, in this kind of setup, as soon as you look like you've officially stopped working, domestic responsibilities can quickly come crashing in: 'the lawn needs mowing'; 'there's a whole pile of laundry in the bathroom'; 'it's your turn to look after the kids'.

Here's an idea for you...

Close your eyes if you want to, but try not to fall asleep. Empty your head of all worries and totally relax your muscles. Be at one with the sounds and smells around you. Keep your breathing shallow, but regular. Yes, what we're talking about here is a form of meditation – and any form of this you can get into is a good thing.

It's also hard sometimes to synchronise your 'nothing' time with everything else that's going on around you. You might want to just lie on the couch and snooze for a moment, or read a good book. Someone else might want to watch TV in the same space or play a noisy computer game. Don't put up with this. It's vitally important to find a space where you can literally do nothing and empty your head a bit – and if that means saying 'Bugger off. I was here first', then so be it.

Creativity is a draining business and it's also a little bit 'Zen' (as we keep mentioning), so it's important that you enter and exit this world in a state of relative calm and peace. If you don't believe us, think about brainstorming sessions you've had in the past. We're willing to bet that the most effective ones happened when you were fresh and at ease, and your head was filled at first with, well, nothing. They will also probably have lasted less than two hours. Anything longer than that and things don't come easily. You get tired. You're head is probably spinning and you really do need a rest. You need to find a space where you can literally do nothing and...

God bless those people who can work creatively for more than, say, four hours at a stretch. But most of us will actually find that four hours of genuine creative endeavour is a good day's work. The rest of the day can be filled nicely with admin, basic grunt-work, socialising, new research – and resting (i.e. doing nothing).

Men of a certain age will probably think of this as 'shed time', and indeed it is helpful to ring-fence a space of your own. But sheds are usually about pottering, and even that is not allowed in this exercise. We really do want you to just sit or lie down in the sun and simply take in the world around you.

It doesn't matter where you are: if it's only twenty minutes in the steam room at the local gym, take the time to just sit there silently, with nothing whatsoever going on inside your head. Curiously this is actually a great way of generating fresh ideas, because for sure something strange will creep into your head at these moments anyway. Just don't be tempted to take those ideas any further straight away. Remember – you're busy doing nothing right now. And tomorrow is another day.

If you absolutely, positively can't put this idea down, then flip back to IDEA 49, *Come back in the morning*, and remind yourself how to put things on the back burner – and take a break.

Try another idea...

'You must have a room or a certain hour of the day or so where you do not know what was in the morning paper...a place where you can simply experience and bring forth what you are, and what you might be...At first you may find nothing's happening.'
JOSEPH CAMPBELL

Defining idea...

231

Q **I simply don't have time to do nothing. Do you expect me to drop everything and ignore all my deadlines just on your say-so?**

A *If you feel like your days are completely jam-packed, and our guess is that perhaps you do, it's more than likely that you're not organising your time very effectively. We also suspect that you're in danger of burning out or falling victim to stress-related diseases. Here's one way to put a check on how busy you are. Make a doctor's appointment even though you're not feeling ill. A general health check-up is always a good thing, and your doctor will not think you are wasting his or her time – honest. The real test here is whether you actually bother to make and keep that appointment. It isn't urgent. It isn't essential. But can you make time for it? If you do manage to, you've not only reassured us that you're committed to staying healthy – you've proved to yourself that you can make time for other things if you put your mind to it.*

Q **Nobody's going to pay me to sit around doing nothing. Would you?**

A *It's true that bosses and clients quite like to pay by the kilo in terms of output. But perhaps you need to be a bit more hard-arsed about how you charge for your time. Make it clear how your time is divided between thinking time, development time, proposal and paperwork time, production time and people time. If you really spell out to people where the value lies, you'll be surprised at how understanding they can be.*

233

The end...

Or is it a new beginning? We hope that the ideas in this book will have inspired you to try some new things. You should be well on your way to a more creative, inspired you, brimming with ideas and inventive ambition.

You're mean, you're motivated and you don't care who knows it.

So why not let us know all about it? Tell us how you got on. What did it for you – what helped you beat that blank page with ideas that fizz? Maybe you've got some tips of your own you want to share (see next page if so). And if you liked this book you may find we have even more brilliant ideas that could change other areas of your life for the better.

You'll find the Infinite Ideas crew waiting for you online at www.infideas.com.

Or if you prefer to write, then send your letters to:
Unleash your creativity
The Infinite Ideas Company Ltd
36 St Giles, Oxford, OX1 3LD, United Kingdom

We want to know what you think, because we're all working on making our lives better too. Give us your feedback and you could win a copy of another *52 Brilliant Ideas* book of your choice. Or maybe get a crack at writing your own.

Good luck. Be brilliant.

Offer one

CASH IN YOUR IDEAS

We hope you enjoy this book. We hope it inspires, amuses, educates and entertains you. But we don't assume that you're a novice, or that this is the first book that you've bought on the subject. You've got ideas of your own. Maybe our author has missed an idea that you use successfully. If so, why not send it to yourauthormissedatrick@infideas.com, and if we like it we'll post it on our bulletin board. Better still, if your idea makes it into print we'll send you four books of your choice or the cash equivalent. You'll be fully credited so that everyone knows you've had another Brilliant Idea.

Offer two

HOW COULD YOU REFUSE?

Amazing discounts on bulk quantities of Infinite Ideas books are available to corporations, professional associations and other organisations.

For details call us on:
+44 (0)1865 514888
Fax: +44 (0)1865 514777
or e-mail: info@infideas.com

235

Where it's at...

brilliant ideas

Unleash your creativity is published by Infinite Ideas, publishers of the acclaimed **52 Brilliant Ideas** series. With the **52 Brilliant Ideas** series you can enhance your existing skills or knowledge with negligible investment of time or money and can substantially improve your performance or know-how of a subject over the course of a year. Or day. Or month. The choice is yours. There are more than 45 titles published in subject areas as diverse as: health & relationships; sports, hobbies & games; lifestyle & leisure and careers, finance & personal development. To learn more, to join our mailing list or to find out about discounts and special offers visit www.infideas.com, or e-mail info@infideas.com.

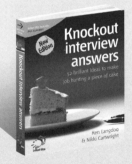